For Better And Worse

Short Stories and Tantalizing Tales:
From Coast to Coast

By Jessica B. Sokol

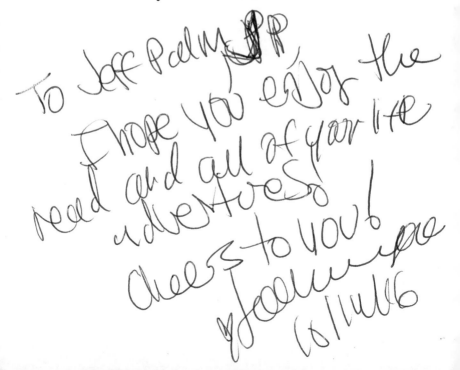

To Jeff Palm JP
I hope you enjoy the read and all of your life adventures
cheers to you!
Jennifer
6/14/16

For my dad, David Sokol, the editor of this book.
And for my mom…

…an unintentional study about men and sexual relations in 2016.

TABLE OF CONTENTS

PREFACE

"Enjoy yourself, it's later than you think."
—sung by Todd Snider (written by Herbert
Magidson and Carl Sigman)

I don't remember how it all started, but I developed a big crush on Portland, Oregon. As a young hopeless romantic in the new millennium, hell-bent on taking chances, I feel I have little to lose and nothing to hide, moving across the country from Western Massachusetts to the Rose City, more or less on a whim.

Have you ever wanted to push yourself to new personal limits to see what and who you may find without a close support system? Or test how successful you can be on your own, how much you can endure? Maybe you will be pleasantly surprised by how much you can trust the good in people you don't know, or come to terms with

1

how disastrously disappointing many really are. Maybe you will see how many daring scenarios you can get out of safely before realizing that this can't last forever, that nothing satisfying is truly working in your favor. Through this journey I keep looking for answers, keep hoping something will change. It becomes a downward spiral too hard to hold on to. And just when I think it's too late, I find something to grab onto, not knowing if I can climb back.

From the suave businessman who abandons me on Valentine's Day in a San Francisco Westin penthouse to a dear friend back home who succumbs to cancer way too young, and from the grubbiest housemate imaginable to the man I inexplicably fall in love with, all kinds of characters join the party—from a soulless fuck to a very special friend. These chapters are filled with candid, real-life experiences, and with coming to grips with disappointments big and small.

Many men I have relations with have a common denominator, despite their varying ages, careers, and backgrounds. None of them are truly *bad* guys, but there are parallels in the ways they treat relationships and how they feel entitled, especially when it comes to women. I learn that most of them, despite their very different exteriors, are good for juicy sex, and sometimes that's all they seem to really want to give… or take.

It becomes a pattern I never quite want to accept, as I remain open-minded on this roller coaster ride to find friendship and love. I write these stories with passion, sincerity, a touch of silliness, and an unquenchable thirst for meaning, with shots of Jameson on the side.

It begins when I close my women's jewelry boutique in Northampton, Massachusetts, leads to a hiking expedition through Israel, and ultimately lands me in Portland with three suitcases and a 26-year-old spirit eager to embrace the moment. I can't help it... I've always loved to travel. By the time I was 15, I'd already seen a good bit of Western Europe, several exotic islands, and much of the United States. I was the first person in my small rural high school to go 1,500 miles away to college. The seeds were sown.

When I have the opportunity to first visit the alluring city of Portland in 2011, the Old Town sign, all lit up on the Burnside Bridge as I arrive downtown, gives me goose bumps and a smile the size of my face. I have an unshakable feeling that this town is beckoning me, and I can't wait to move here.

I fly back east after that visit with just one thing on my mind: to move and move quickly. But just a month before leaving with my one-way ticket to Portland International Airport, an historic late-October snowstorm hits our cozy Western Massachusetts town, causing prolonged blackouts up and down the coast. My favorite people in the world (my family) and I hole up inside for days with no hot water or electricity, and it's really cold. We cannot take showers and are bundled up in coats and blankets day and night. It's perpetually dark, and outside, everything's shut down.

Halloween is canceled for the first time in decades, and we drink lots of whiskey to stay warm. We play Hangman by candlelight like in the olden days, and my phrases to be solved are things like "Portland Party People" and "Portland Rocks." I am ready for something new and have a gut feeling that Portland will be the perfect place for me.

In moving there, my hope is to break free of the chains I felt running a store for the last few years in a depressed economy. I want to embark on a new adventure in Portland and find loyal friends, a comfortable apartment, a job, and feel secure and grounded in this exciting and curious place I am so smitten with. But like that Old Town sign at night on the Burnside Bridge, the allure will dim as the glow fades and the fantasy becomes reality. When the snowstorm clears, I leave for my new adventure across the country.

During my first few weeks in Portland, I keep on running into the same party people (as foreshadowed on those Hangman sticky notes) at various downtown haunts. One night, I meet a cute guy, a friend of a new friend. I don't really know anyone in this rainy city, 3,000 miles from home. But he's particularly witty and attractive, and he buys me drinks. I call him Carter (remember *The O.C.*?). He's in his early 30s, has shaggy dark hair, enticing blue eyes, and he makes me laugh about the seedy but homey country bar we find ourselves in, with slutty servers dancing on the bar and bad karaoke singers coming out of the woodwork.

He takes me home and we end up nicely buzzed and passionately going at each other in his well-kept downtown apartment. We kiss hard coming in the doorway and dance around, making out until we break the big closet we end up leaning against. I think we just might have something going. The last thing I remember is falling comfortably onto his bed.

The next morning I awake, rub my eyes, and gaze sleepily onto his floor-to-ceiling bedroom bookshelf. I think I am having a nightmare. It's filled with thick imposing hardcovers including George W. Bush's autobiography and some other Republican mythology. I feel a bit queasy and call a cab. I have to get out of here immediately. Carter tries to contact me, but we don't speak again. That bookshelf told me more than enough. There has to be better taste in this city.

During my years in Portland there are more downs than ups, as might be expected from such an impulsive plan. The city knocks me down, kicks my ass, is messy at times, and changes my perspective on pretty much everything I think I know. One evening I fall walking home from my office downtown. Roundtrip, I walked five miles a day to work during my time in Portland, and I still have a big purple scar on my left knee to show for it.

Portland never let me live easily. Now, a few years later, back in the Northeast three time zones away, this book revisits some unsettling times. That mark on my leg is a reminder of strength, of picking myself up off the pavement and making it home. It's also a permanent reminder of some not-so glory days.

Throughout these stories, my parents play their own humorous roles, plying me with advice and strength from afar. The close bonds I make with people from around the globe during my time in Portland are also chronicled here. Thanks to them, the brutal times are bearable, even the bad times are good. I can sometimes chuckle now about the jerks who weaseled their way in and out of my life, and this is all why I wrote *For Better And Worse*. As Bruce Springsteen once said, "Someday we'll look back on this and it will all seem funny." La la la.

In the end, there is an unexpected love story that remains a mystery as I ponder how my life will unfold. So just like the men in these stories, and just like the city itself, the challenge of making a relationship I hope will work seems almost impossible. It's one last enduring punch Portland serves up to me as I want to leave it.

While these tales are all honest and true, some of the names have been changed to spare the guilty more embarrassment than they've already caused themselves. I hope you enjoy taking this bumpy ride with me and find the inspiration to take chances, stick things out, be adventurous, and find love. And, for better and worse, laugh along the way.

CHAPTER 1

THE ISRAEL TRIP, AN OLYMPIC SWIMMER, AND THE MILE-HIGH CLUB

"Congratulations honey, you're one of us now!"
—The male flight attendant from Tel Aviv to New York City

I was so overdue for something new. Oddly intrigued by Portland, Oregon, I read about the city's vegan bars, food carts, and clothing designers in my free time while working 11-hour days at the boutique I owned in Massachusetts. I desperately wanted to get out. The hopeless romantic in me talked to my lame boyfriend at the time about moving across the country, but he wasn't interested, and growing less interesting by the minute. My friends compared him to a washed-out, half-dead, vampire type in *Twilight*.

My upscale women's jewelry and accessories store had a prime location inside the shopping center in downtown Northampton. My store was known for importing one-of-a-kind jewelry and glass goods from Israel and Italy, and I worked with designers from New York and California. Everything sparkled when you walked by the windows, and it was even more breathtaking once you stepped inside.

I love the city of Northampton more than words can describe. From Bob Dylan concerts at the Pines Theater in Look Park to the latest independent films showing at Pleasant Street Theater, and from campaigning for Democrats downtown to seeing my favorite authors including Augusten Burroughs at local bookstores, I was smitten with this city.

Many consider Northampton the lesbian capital of the world, and it's dotted with top-notch restaurants and music venues. I was nine months old when I attended my first concert. It was comedian Steven Wright at the cozy Iron Horse Coffeehouse. Apparently I gurgled, and I'm told he responded by commenting something like, "My, the fans are getting younger all the time."

Northampton is friendly, artsy, liberal, and the place I call home. The town is full of progressives and old-timers, and it's only a short ride from five big-time colleges: University of Massachusetts, Amherst; Amherst College; Hampshire College; Mount Holyoke College; and Smith College, a stone's throw from downtown. Some theorize these schools were the inspiration for *Scooby-Doo* characters.

I had the ideal apartment, directly across the street from my shop (and less than a two-minute walk to the ever-bustling Northampton Brewery), and a full social life here in the Pioneer Valley. In March 2011, with my store lease about to expire, I decide to sell everything I have left in the shop.

Frankly, I couldn't wait to be done dealing with the cold-hearted building managers here. Management changed hands while I owned my store, and shops that had been in business 20 years were shutting down. It was no longer a shopping hotspot for tourists or locals, and it was far more depressing for me to pay absurdly high rent in a stagnant spot.

Management started treating many of the small-business owners as mall corporation store-tenders, mandating long hours even on the slowest of days when they couldn't hold their end of the bargain with a desirable space to rent. Drug addicts were regularly being hauled out of the building, and my store suffered theft monthly. It fucking sucked.

The sixty-something owner of a lovely flower shop across from mine left early every night to tend to her ailing husband at home. The powers that be caught up with her in the parking garage one night, insisting she vacate her space and close her business despite doing respectable numbers and paying her pricey rent on time.

For two months, construction in a shop soon to open next to mine created so much dust and pounding noise that customers were driven away, and my sales declined. Still, management couldn't find it in them to give me a break on my rent. So I started scanning the Internet for a new city to live in, a new adventure to embark upon.

I stuck it out through the duration of my lease, but was fed up. By the end, I quickly sublet my apartment and broke up with that lame boyfriend. This chapter in my life was coming to an end, and it couldn't happen soon enough.

It was hard to turn away from the once-bustling store I put everything of myself into. But it was not hard to let go of something I never really felt I had control of in the first place, even though it was mine. I would be the one still paying off my business loan for years to come, and the space would be taken over by others who couldn't make it work over time. Poor management of this building was not changing.

But I am out! It feels as if the whole world is opening up for me. I'd been working seven days a week for the last couple years, and opportunities now seem endless. I immediately want to sign up for a Birthright trip to Israel, but funds are slim and the waiting list long, thanks to the Bernie Madoff scandal.

Luckily, just before I reach the cut-off age of 26, an Israel Outdoors trip opens with a hiking opportunity. Knowing it could be my last chance to go, I take it. But I'm no casual hiker, I don't even work out. My idea of exercise is walking everywhere in the city I live in and having sex. In any case, I know this Israel experience is one I cannot pass up...

This trip turns out to be different from any Birthright trip I'd ever heard about from friends.

Our tour guide with blond dreads and some accent I can't figure out thinks he's training us for the Israeli military. His masochistic idea of a "little hike" is an entire day climbing uphill on jagged rocks to an abandoned Syrian bunker, with iron fences and landmines on either side. And when he takes us to the Syrian border, we have to be evacuated during our lunch of street falafels because of a mass shooting at the gates. Then there's the time we have to camp in flimsy tents in the Negev Desert among the scorpions and similarly terrifying creatures. Meanwhile, I realize the concepts of "mean girls" and gender double standards are alive and well in my cluster of American strangers. This is quite surprising and disappointing, especially from fellow Jews. I expect more from them.

The second night there, I find myself in a kibbutz in Northern Israel partying in a legit bomb-shelter pub with our group. The sweet 18-year-old boy bartender tells me he loves my voice when I order a Jameson neat, and he pours everything left in the bottle into a highball glass for me. The wonders of a friendly accent from a high-pitched American.

A very tall, cute, blue-eyed guy comes up behind me and says he's never seen anyone get such good service so quickly in a crowded bar line, except for him. He lives in Portland (coincidently), works with computers, and used to swim with Michael Phelps. I call him Olympic. We chat and drink and kiss, and the next thing I know after that highball of Jamo, we've decided to leave. I can't walk straight, and this six-foot seven-inch athlete with a good Jewish head of hair scoops me up and carries me out. It's quite dark, and we don't know our way around the compound. The next thing I do know, I'm practically in a ditch on top of him. We'd fallen off a ledge, I smacked my head, he hurt his ankle, and I don't care about anything except fucking him right then and there.

We have sex that night in and on many inappropriate places where two nice Jewish kids on a kibbutz in Northern Israel should not be. Like on a late-model pickup, in the dining hall, and back in his room, where he has roommates. I remember the chill of the truck's hood as I am flat on my back with my legs wrapped around him in front of me. And being naked on top of him on the dining room lobby floor as he's grabbing my ass, and me nervously thinking that there must be cameras everywhere.

I like this guy, but we hang out with different groups of friends throughout the journey. Near the end of the trip, we arrive in Jerusalem. This is by far my favorite city in Israel because of the incredible street markets, museums, culture, bars, people, food, warm weather, and not too much hiking. I recall a poignant picture that Alex, one of the kindhearted girlfriends I met on the trip, took of my hand on top of Olympic's hand in the National Cemetery after we'd just visited the Holocaust Museum. There are moments like that you'll not soon forget.

The night before we head back to New York is blurred with hookah hits, vodka shots, and dancing. I wake up in Olympic's bed again, and happy. I proposition him for an adventure on our plane ride home, and he's a little shy about it... at first.

I love flying, especially internationally because of the free wine and beer. My flight attendant on this trip particularly likes me, and when we all realize the Hasidic Jews are about to delay our scheduled 13-hour flight with sundown prayers before takeoff, he hooks me up with boxes of wine under my seat. A couple hours in, I write Olympic a note and go in search of him in the privileged section up front. (Super-tall people get such cool perks sometimes.)

I find him asleep and leave the note on his chest. A little while later, I'm feeling quite buzzed as I am one of only three people in my entire section awake, chatting, and examining the map of the countries we're flying over. I don't know if Olympic came back to find me at that point or just had to stretch, but I run into him in the aisle. I grab his hand and lead him to the handicap bathroom, escaping the terrifying Israeli woman flight attendant in the back who's already lost her temper once at a passenger attempting to get to the bathroom during take-off.

Joining the mile-high club is tricky with two normal-size people, but it's particularly challenging when one of them is 6' 7". I did plan for the occasion, though, and wore a hot pink dress that requires no bra or underwear for that matter. Once you figure out the logistics, you can both come pretty easily and enjoyably. I remember reading in

Psychology Today that the back of an airplane is one of the most desirable places to fuck due to atmospheric pressure, and because your sense of pleasure is heightened by the intimacy and eroticism of it all. It was, indeed... with mile-high-club mission accomplished.

Once I get back to my seat, incredibly satisfied with myself, my gem of a flight attendant comes up to me with a little box. He says, "I saw you go back to the bathroom with that handsome man. There's only one reason two people would ever go in there together. Congratulations honey, you're one of us now!" He hands me the box containing a pair of plastic pilot wings. Best gift ever.

A few hours later, I want to do it again, and Olympic smiles in agreement. The guys I know from our journey through Israel are giving me high-fives, and most of the girls are giving me the same piss-poor scowls they did all trip. But I am high on life from the complete Israel experience. And I earned a second pair of plastic wings on that flight, which I happily give to Olympic when I visit him on my first trip to Portland later that summer. He'd earned them too.

Back at JFK, my good friend Dave from Northampton picks me up at the airport and says that despite all the Hasidic Jews he sees coming through the Tel Aviv arrival terminal, it is the girl, surrounded by people and kissing this very tall man, who is causing a scene. He knew it had to be me. I proceed to say goodbye to everyone and head out to the airport parking lot, happy to be back home. I'd made some good friends on this journey, and of course, there's Olympic.

I'm quite giddy from being sleep deprived while hiking and camping throughout Israel—thank goodness for the hummus, olives, dates, and vodka—as I chat away about my trip. I finally pass out in Dave's passenger seat. When we arrive in Northampton three hours later, I can sense it and wake up immediately. I try to convince him to hit the Brewery, not realizing it's 9 o'clock the next morning here.

Not long after the Israel trip, I visit Olympic in Portland and fall in love with the city. I knew a world filled with veganism, farmers' markets, microbreweries, hippies, hipsters, and plenty of successful young people would be a place I could live next. It was a memorable and crazy week exploring the city, enjoying great bars with new people, and going to a mansion party in Lake Oswego that resulted in an overnight trip to Seaside Beach. Even the non-stop rain throughout the trip couldn't deter me from being infatuated with this place.

Flying back home to Massachusetts after getting my first taste of Portland, I know I want to move to Oregon for a month, maybe a year, maybe five. A few weeks after my vacation there, I pack three suitcases and buy a one-way ticket across the country, with no set apartment or job or true friends there. I had successfully figured out where my next life adventure would take me, and I have my experience in Israel to thank for that.

Coincidentally, the job I end up getting in downtown Portland is right across the street from Olympic's high-rise apartment on the waterfront. Our friendship continues, and his location makes for some excellent lunchtime afternoon delights. On solid ground.

That oh-so-familiar line—about when something happens in a certain place, it stays there—simply isn't true about Israel and me. Not for a minute.

Israel… Massachusetts… Portland. I know this airborne wanderlust is propelling me to where I want to go next. And I have the wings to prove it.

CHAPTER 2

THE KEARNEY CURSE

"What do I do with them?"
—The asshole housemate from Ghana, mumbling about the dirty pots and pans he leaves out on the kitchen stove

My trip out to live in Portland in late 2011 was a nightmare, but I was in such high spirits that the flight delays in each of the two cities I transferred in didn't phase me. I'd already been in the Portland mindset for weeks, so it was like "Just fucking get me there already!" I had a temporary apartment that I'd found on Craigslist waiting for me for the first month. It was in Northwest, near 21st and Flanders, a trendy area with bars and nice shops. I'd read that Northwest 21st and 23rd Streets are fun places to venture, located just outside the Pearl District downtown.

The woman renting out her room was on her way to India for at least a month, if not permanently, she advertised and later told me. There were two other housemates, sisters, but only one really stayed there. I called her Scout. She has an adorable dog, and we'd Skype when I was still in Massachusetts. We hit it off, and she is a good friend to me as soon as we meet in person. Together we'd soon frequent McMenamins Blue Moon Tavern for happy hour, tater tots, and their cozy fireplace. We'd have *Modern Family* marathons and talk on and on about music, men, and Portland.

Upon arrival, I knew Olympic of course, and we remained friends. But it was really Olympic's buddy, an intriguing man I'd met at the mansion party in Lake Oswego that summer and spent a promising weekend with at the beach, who strongly encouraged my move. Olympic had certainly given us his blessing. Mansion Party Man and I had been talking every day since we met, and it seemed things between us just might lead somewhere. At least he led me to believe that.

He's the one who met me at the airport when I arrived in Portland with my three suitcases, several hundred dollars, and an open mind. He helped me settle in, and we spent my first weekend there together. He turned out to be a letdown after all the hype. And he was wicked lame in bed.

After my first couple days living in Portland, I meet more than one woman with whom he's been sleeping around. I never expected anything romantically exclusive with the schmuck, but over

18

the phone he'd enthusiastically counted down the days until I arrived, giving me false hope he really was excited to see me again. And he promised to show me around and have my back in this new city 3,000 miles from home. He didn't follow through at all after that first weekend, and I felt quite lost.

I come to terms with the fact that Mansion Party Man is more of a sleazy, lying, douche bag… to put it nicely. After this hits home, I call him out, he comes up with some lame excuse about being depressed in the winter, and we never speak again. I see his raunchy escapades on Facebook (not looking depressed at all) and quickly unfriend him. Surprisingly I only see him one more time, from a distance, here in Portland. I like to think he contracted multiple venereal diseases from one too many nights singing karaoke at Dixie (a country bar he frequents, with half-naked bartenders dancing on the counters) and sleeping with underage sluts, and that he was forced to live under the radar for a while. Or something like that.

That first apartment I move into is very comfortable with Scout, until the second week when the woman who's supposed to be on her way to India fails to get her visa, and just shows up at the apartment. No hello, no nothing. Except she wants to know what the hell is wrong with the shower's hot water. Umm, what? She ends up spending the entire month on the couch while I stay in the bedroom I paid her for.

Papers were signed, rent was paid, and she has no right to be here. She is dirty in the kitchen, leaves clothes all over her "room," aka the living room, and is the complete epitome of a spoiled bitch. Scout, too, is appalled. We both move out around the same time after that roller-coaster ride of a month.

The only comic relief was when the stupid bitch's car got broken into while parked right outside the apartment, where she never should've been. After four weeks of starting to ponder why the hell I moved to Portland in the first place, I have to find a second apartment in this unfamiliar city.

I have lived in odd situations before, but nothing as painfully awkward as that first month in Portland. As of yet, anyway. I long for the days in my brownstone in Dublin when one of my best friends, Patrick, whom I met while living abroad, would barge into my bedroom at 6 a.m., having just returned home from The George, a gay downtown bar.

He'd hop into bed with me and fill me in on far too many details of his latest one-night stand. I also dream of the days when I had my living spaces all set up for me, like in college when Lynn University would put Honors students in comfy hotel rooms with nearby pools and room service. And I really wish I could afford a place of my own, like back in Northampton, but that was clearly out of the question considering I have no job yet.

My first job interview is at what I thought would be an ideal boutique in which to work, but I walk out even before the interview is over. It's clear that after owning my own store, certain managers and I might not get along so well. That, and um, Portland fashion is kind of an oxymoron.

I do grow to love the fashion in Portland, but it's just clear that retail would never be for me again. My dad told me he was spending my wedding fund on my jobless ass thus far in my move, and I told him it's a good thing I don't ever plan to get married. That conversation almost ended there, but he told me I really had to get a job soon, seriously. It was hard to explain to him how it wasn't that easy.

I move into my second apartment right off 21st and Kearney, pretty close to my first one in Northwest, and these places, while safe, are not cheap. I would be the fourth roommate in this second living situation. There's an odd couple and another roommate in this three-bedroom place. And a cat named Cherb. Right away I hit it off with the single roommate. She's from Sri Lanka, works at Oregon Health & Science University (OHSU), is smart and sweet, and we start drinking wine together. Turns out we have much in common, from not really understanding Portland, to Luke Perry being our first crush back in the day. She's like my older sister from across the world whom I'm finally getting to meet.

I call her Nomads because she's rarely home, and soon our friendship becomes inevitably deeper when we cannot stand the couple we live with. They are in their mid-30s; he is from Ghana, she is a mystery, and they have a very peculiar relationship.

He sleeps all day, she somehow manages the entire apartment complex we live in, and they turn out to be the biggest slobs I have ever known.

It all starts when I wake up, sleepy and slightly hung-over, my first morning there. My dresser handles are half super-glued on, my suitcases barely in my room, but I'd had a fun night out. I venture out to the kitchen to make breakfast. The day before, I spent a good chunk of change on groceries for myself, and when I approach the kitchen, it's a grotesque mess. And by mess, I mean pure filth in the most unsanitary ways. This didn't even resemble the apartment I had been shown. There are chicken bones strewn on the counters, butter dripping out of the container onto the microwave, and pizza boxes everywhere. There are dirty dishes piled so high in the sink you can't use the faucet. And most of my groceries are no longer where I put them in the fridge.

In college, I had a bet with my dad that if I could go four full semesters without getting sick from drinking, he'd give me $1,000. I ended up losing a couple times and we lowered the stakes, but in the end, I earned about $400 after I came home from my Ireland semester without vomiting. That was in 2005, and never once did I get sick from drinking again. Now, from my utter disgust in this foul kitchen, in the morning still feeling a little buzzed, I run to the toilet and throw up. My vegan eyes and fuzzy head could not take the grubbiness, and my seven-year vomit-free stretch literally goes down the drain.

Nomads, who'd already lived here a couple months, says this happens from time to time, that the sink is always a mess. She cooks here. It doesn't really bother her because she's staying at her boyfriend's place most of the time. Lucky her, but I can't live like this.

I sense apartment number three in my future. I leave notes, try to communicate with the couple about cleanliness and respectable shared spaces, but they turn out to be impossible to reason with. I start to lose it when the 33-year-old man from Ghana—who can't fucking clean up anything in the kitchen or living room—has to make breakfast during the same 10 minutes I do. There are food-caked dirty pots and pans everywhere and they've been accumulating all week. He doesn't appear to have a job, does not clean, cook, or do anything except, well, cheat on his wife as I soon learn. So when I tell him he can't use a burner because his dirty cookware is occupying all the others except the one I'm temporarily using, he gives me a puzzled look, and in his broken English says, "What do I do with them?" I say, "You clean them." He looks at me befuddled and then just shoves them into the oven. He puts the dirty pots and pans into the fucking oven!

The sink is overflowing with their pile of dirty dishes, and he couldn't be bothered with that, so what else is he to do but make more of a mess. The guy's worse then a cheating, messed-up 17-year-old frat boy, and he can't keep his married dick in his pants, hold a job, or clean a pot. Worthless excuse for a human being.

23

I tell Nomads I am moving, and she agrees to come with me. The month does not get better with these low-lifes. It gets worse. We start referring to the place as the Kearney Curse, as the street we live on is Kearney Street.

While we're there, the couple gets a dog, a black Lab much too big for this apartment, without even checking in with Nomads and me about it. Lab runs into my room his first day in the apartment, and I am shocked at this new housemate development. What if Nomads or I are allergic or scared of dogs? It was rather thoughtless, I think, not to ask or inform us about their decision, especially in such a crowded apartment.

They keep Lab locked in a tiny cage where he shits constantly, stinking up the entire place, and they can't take the time to clean up. I despise these people. One day, Ghana slob takes Lab out for a walk and it shits all over the common hallway outside the front door. Dogs are not allowed in the complex, his wife is the manager, and when I say something to her, it's as if I'm annoying her by asking her to clean it up. And well, of course *he* won't do it. Cherb the cat starts peeing everywhere out of sheer terror, and I actually contemplate giving up my security deposit and sleeping in a cheap hotel for the rest of the month.

They have the carpets ripped up for days on end after this, again with no heads-up to Nomads and me. She basically moves into her boyfriend's house until we move together into a new apartment. At one point, I can't even leave my

24

room for about 12 hours because there's furniture blocking my door. And when I tell them this is a problem, they just take down my fucking bedroom door. The noise alone from the work being done causes the worst migraine I ever had, and I realize it's probably a good thing I don't actually have a job yet because I wouldn't be able to get a good night's sleep here. The Ghana slob then screws up our whole Internet system so we are without it for days, making my job search harder. And more shit happens with their poor animals, resulting in Nomads needing to have her cherished bedding dry-cleaned.

I start getting more than annoyed, nervous even, as these housemate assholes are yelling at each other constantly, and I see domestic-violence red flags everywhere. A friend puts a lock on my bedroom door for me, and I keep empty wine bottles by my bedside, just in case. This is freaking NW 21st Street in Portland for fuck's sake, not seamy Gresham, and this is totally unacceptable.

Then one night I am kept up until 5 a.m. Not one, not two, but three of this loser's mistresses show up hooting and hollering until daylight. They are all there, with the equally worthless wife, arguing loudly with the couple about nights out, text messages, phone calls, hotel horseplay, and lots of utter nonsense.

Around 3 o'clock that morning, I go out to say something to these five thoughtless fucks yelling their faces off. But when I walk into the living room where their fat asses are squished together on the couches, the mistresses are all, "Heyyyyy girl! You are so adorable! Sorry to keep ya up like this, but ya know how this shit has to go *down*."

Actually no, I don't. All I can think is that I'm on the set of *Jerry Springer* or *Punked*... and weirdly, they have *Gossip Girl* on in the background. I crack a smile at these jerks, go back to my room, open a bottle of wine, shake my head, and watch *Gilmore Girls* until I finally fall asleep. These fucking morons deserve each other.

The Ghana asshole ends up in jail that night after who knows what happened after I passed out, and the piss-poor wife bails him out the next day. It was so over. The last I heard while moving out is they're trying to move to Ghana and adopt children to bring back to the States. Probably his own, whom he had helped create and then abandoned in a previous encounter in some unknown land. That's all these fucks needed: to raise children.

Thankfully, Nomads' and my days were numbered at the Kearney Curse as we found a new place in Southeast, right off Hawthorne, where we'd soon be moving. But not soon enough. Our new apartment will affectionately be named Pad from here on, as Nomads, in her charming Sri Lankan accent, says one evening, "See you at Pad" instead of "See you at *the* pad."

I didn't spend the last few evenings at Kearney Curse as I was lucky enough to have met a few people to stay with. I also acknowledge that Kearney wasn't all bad as I did meet Nomads there, and she becomes the best roommate I could have wished for during my next 18 months in Portland.

The Kearney Curse helped give me insight into the seedier side of the city, but that exists in all cities. Still, it's a little more sobering when venturing out into the world on your own, especially across the country without really knowing anyone at first. I just keep hoping there will be more decent and trustworthy people than deplorable ones on my journey. I come to accept the fact that some of them might actually make me physically ill, and remind myself of a Latin phrase I heard once: *Illegitimi non carborundum.* Don't let the bastards grind you down.

CHAPTER 3

THE SOGGY HOLIDAYS

"Come hang with us."
—A group of reveling strangers enticing me to join them outside a hookah bar on Christmas Eve

A few weeks after moving to Portland, the holidays are here and I feel alone. My first roommate, Scout, invites me to her mom's place in Eugene for Christmas Eve, and I graciously say no. It's the first time I'll have a night to myself since moving here, and I'm told I can't drink there. A holiday without drinking just doesn't feel like a holiday.

Instead, on Christmas Eve I treat myself to a lovely dinner on Northwest 21st, and then see the film *Shame* playing at Cinema 21, an older, artsy theater. There are three other people in the place, all old men. I actually watch the film this time around; a few months later I will see it again and remember none of it.

Afterward it is dark and getting late, but NW 21st is safe and I feel I should celebrate some sort of holiday cheer before heading home. I walk past a hookah and booze lounge, and a group of strangers are outside, all loud and happy and calling me from the other side of the street. "Come hang with us," a couple of them say in near-unison, waving their hands. Reminding me of the line from *Clueless*, I can't say no. I amble over and take a drag from one of the guys' cigarettes when he offers it to me, and we all head inside. They have two tables and are super friendly. I knew Portland had to have people like this. These friends all work at a delicatessen in town and are enjoying a little holiday time away from their families.

There are three guys and three girls, and I hit it off with them on this festive night. After we close out our tab, the girls go off to some other event and the guys invite me to an apartment. The house party the girls are going to is quite far away, and I didn't want to get stranded far from home. I say yes to the guys because their apartment is right down the street, and I'm getting to know this new neighborhood well. The funniest of the three is wearing a cowboy hat. He looks incredibly handsome as he flirts with me, and I sense I can trust this group. At the apartment, they're chatty and chummy. We smoke weed, drink red wine, and end up at another bar, whose name I quickly forget.

Elton, the one in the cowboy hat, and I are hitting it off. He offers to walk me home after the

29

last bar. I say yes because it is the first time in Portland that I won't have a roommate around, and I want sex. He is gentle and charming, and when I invite him in he is very eager. We end up naked in my bed and start to fuck around. I ask him if he has a condom, and he says no. We are still quite buzzed and I tell him he should go to the market around the corner to get some and come back. He is hesitant to leave but says he really wants me, and agrees to go out. I ask him if he knows how to get there and back. He assures me as he gets dressed.

I tell him to ring the bell when he gets back, and I lock the front door. I don't know if I doze off or he gets lost, but I wake up a few hours later and it's just starting to get light out. He never came back. It's drizzling outside... it seems to always be raining here. It dawns on me that no market would possibly be open to sell condoms at 3 o'clock on Christmas morning, but we hadn't thought of that. I'm sure he tried. We also didn't exchange numbers, and I never see him again. Merry Christmas to me. But oh well...

A week after that somewhat disappointing Christmas Eve, it's New Year's Eve 2011. I decide to walk to the Mission Theater. It's a McMenamins venue that has everything from *Portlandia* showings every Friday to presidential debates on their movie screen. And plenty of live shows too: from Jeff Garland comedy stand-up to burlesque. On New Year's Eve, it is the perfect place for me to go when I don't have other plans, and Scout assures me I will love it. It's also close to home.

Since this is my fourth week in Portland, I still don't know many people. Scout is staying in with videos, and I really want to party. My Special Friend, a sweet guy I met my first week in Portland, is quickly becoming my closest buddy here, but he's with his kids this evening. (Ours is a platonic friendship, nothing more.) And I really don't want to hang out with anyone from the downtown club scene tonight.

Members of Modest Mouse are playing at the Mission Theater, as is Talkdemonic, a duo that plays crazy music that sounds like hardcore-techno meets Celtic-roots. There are strobe lights, but their violin playing and singing makes me feel like they should be in some sort of gastropub setting in Ireland. It is weird, so very Portland, and I love them and their music. I develop a crush on the girl playing violin. She has long dark hair with bangs and really rocks on the string instruments.

I meet a couple girls, also by themselves this chilly night at the bar. And at midnight, all warm and boozy, these fun strangers and I count down, kiss each other, laugh, and enjoy ourselves while dancing to the music. I am having a successful first New Year's Eve here in Portland, as sad and lonely as that might sound.

I catch a man eyeing me from behind as I order another drink from the bar. He approaches me. When we start talking, he tells me how beautiful I look and asks to dance. I meet a few of his friends, and around 2 a.m. tell him I should walk home. He offers to come with me, and I tell him I live very close. He insists, and I like that.

When we get to my front door he asks to kiss me, and I say yes. I give him my phone number, and he texts later that night and the next day.

He owns a place far out in Southeast Portland that I will frequent many times, and he bikes to work downtown every day. He's older than me, has a successful business career, and turns out to be quite decent in bed. He has a nerdy look that isn't unappealing, quite thin, brunette hair, glasses, and I like how much he knows his way around the city. He's not physically my type, but I really want to meet some good men. He has a two-story house, an extensive wine collection, and enjoys his privacy when not out and about.

We go out a few times but don't always agree on things to do. Like trivia. I love it, he can't stand it. One time he takes me to a German bar called Victory. I make a reference to Drama's infamous line in *Entourage* quoting "Victory!" and he pooh-poohs it, saying he never saw the show. He's also dismissive about the fact this bar doesn't have vegan entrees. But for the most part, we get along nicely.

For a few months we hang out, drink, eat, have sleepovers, and talk a lot. I meet his two best friends, a gay couple that I quickly adore. Once, we all go to Silverado, a male strip club in Portland, and somehow I lose a very expensive and sentimental Mary Francis scarf from my Northampton shop to a stripper. Another time, we all go to Boxxes, another gay club with television screens showing nothing but naked men's asses. Linguini, the man I am sleeping with, even suggests we go there just the two of us one time. He said it was for the drink specials, which is fine with me. In the meantime, Linguini, me, and his down-to-earth gay friends frequent bars around the city—from Virginia Café, an intimate, divey spot that has been around since the early 1900s to Departure, an upscale, trendy lounge at the top of The Nines Hotel. It's all very fun.

Then one chilly night we all go to an outdoor Southeast bar with heat lamps. Linguini is clearly intoxicated, and I am trying to have a good time with his friends in the cold and non-stop rain. He gets loud and belligerent and his friends tell him they'll call him a cab. I even offer to go home with him, but he doesn't want that. In fact, even after all these weeks of connecting with him, out of the blue he drunkenly blurts, "I don't even care about you, Jess." Just like that, in the middle of a bar, in front of his friends. What decent guy says that to someone he's been inside?

I am befuddled. And hurt. His friends call him a cab and take me to another bar and tell me what a worthless piece of shit he is being. I appreciate that. They say he has a temper sometimes when he's drunk, not that it's an excuse. I was never that smitten with Linguini, but he was pretty good company for a while, and I thought he might be a reliable friend.

Linguini texts me the next day saying how sorry he is. I ask him why he acted like such a fool and he responds with some lame excuse that cannot defend his behavior, and he doesn't know what got into him. I sense latent anger issues, or maybe he's gay himself and for some reason has not quite accepted it yet. I know one thing: my New Year's wish of finding friendship and love here isn't coming true anytime soon.

CHAPTER 4

THE WESTIN

"Please just take it for the cab ride home."
—The Westin

One rainy Thursday night there's a Facebook pandemic from promoters of a black-out celebration at a club called Dirty. I go because I don't yet have a job here, don't have to wake up early the next day, and love a good party. Why not? This downtown club scene hasn't grown on me, but when asked to go by a couple people I know from my post-Israel vacation here, I jump at the opportunity.

I wear a dress I got in Paris—satin tutu-like bottom up to here, sparkly black plunging neckline down to there—and a white fuzzy hat because it's January and it'll make my big blue eyes pop. That should take some attention off my breasts and legs in this dress, or so I tell myself.

As soon as I walk into the place, a very attractive man at the bar, about 35, hones in on me like a guided missile. I want him immediately as he reminds me of an American Jude Law-type. He says he knows the owner, isn't a big fan of the club, is in Portland on business, and insists on buying me drinks. He can't keep his eyes off me. He asks me to dance and we do. We start smooching, and soon I've lost the friends I came with. I'm not crazy about the wannabe strippers dancing on poles, and am a little put off to see the douche bag, Mansion Party Man, out of the corner of my eye.

This new man at the bar, the gorgeous stranger of a businessman, buys me one Jameson, then another, and asks me to leave with him to go to the Spin Room next door. I say no because I don't know what the Spin Room is, and I'm still thinking I might hook back up with the people I came with. But a couple hours later and after one too many LMFAO songs, he asks me to go to his room in the downtown Portland Westin. I say yes.

In the morning my new friend, who I call Westin, wakes me by kissing me as he's getting out of our huge, white, plush bed overlooking the city, at least 10 floors high. I'm naked and happy and reminded of our night just looking at the mini-bar bottles and condoms strewn around the room. I hear him getting into the shower, and I sleepily roll out of bed and follow him in. He smiles as he sees me get inside the glass with him, and everything that happens in that beautiful shower is as sexy as you might imagine. Afterward, he dries

36

me off, wraps me in a super-soft oversize robe, tucks me back into bed, and tells me to go back to sleep. He calls the front desk and extends the check-out time for me as he dresses in his Brooks Brothers suit and Cole Haan shoes. I am content, actually euphoric, in the moment.

He kisses me on the lips and forehead and whispers that he's going to leave some money by the television for my cab ride home. I insist he shouldn't, but after he leaves I see cash on the bedside table. He also leaves behind his favorite Pringle sweater that he got in Edinburgh, and I remember telling him I didn't want to take a cab in the middle of the rainy afternoon in my sparkly black and silver party dress from the night before. Broadway Cab has always seen me at my finest.

I call my dad. I want to know if I have legit gone from Portland party girl to someone who may have just been paid for sex. My dad says, "Enjoy that cozy bed! The money is for a cab, you don't have a job there yet. He gets it." I don't think my dad realizes that the slush fund is 10 times more than the cab would cost that day. And there *was* that ridiculous hot and steamy shower...

This was my first time staying at the Portland Westin, but definitely not the last. Though I didn't know it at the time, Westin will be back soon. The very next weekend he surprises me, calling to say he's just flown in from Southern California, where he lives, and wants to see me. He says he has a business dinner meeting, and we agree to meet later at my favorite Irish bar downtown.

It is raining and chilly, and I wait for him at the bar for what feels like forever. I assume he's probably drinking shots in the Pearl District at Blue Hour on his business dinner. I'm okay though. My bartender is around his age, with piercing blue eyes, and he's definitely eye-fucking me as I patiently wait.

Westin eventually shows up and slides next to me at the bar, kisses me intensely, and quickly orders us both top-shelf Scotch from the vast liquor library. He tells me he loves the live music and this bar I chose. We talk about where we attended college, our families, our career plans, passions, studying abroad in Europe—him in Scotland, me in Ireland—and we can't keep our hands off each other. It's romantically obnoxious.

He then tells me he wasn't supposed to come here to Portland for this meeting, but he had to see me again immediately. This leads to him promptly paying our bill and us taking a short cab ride back to the downtown Westin.

That night he opens up about his two kids but never gives a straight answer as to whether he's still married, or for that matter ever was. And this initiates a long discussion of how that is even possible. He says, "I want to make sure you are okay with all this."

I don't know if I am, or what I'm supposed to be okay with. I'm a little taken aback, perplexed, yet I tell him I am open to explanation, but I might want to go home that night. He understands, throws me some Ketel One nips from the mini bar, and we keep talking.

He explains how he never had a wedding, but rather a common-law ceremony for his family's sake, and that everything with his "ex-wife," who is now more of a "friend," is over. Their families are connected, and I assume that has something to do with money and his kids. He's a successful lawyer, regularly in Portland these days, trying to close a deal with a pharmaceutical company here. Fucking lawyers. The mini vodka bottles and his honesty sway me to stay, which leads to some hardcore sex and another heated Westin shower, which in turn leads to another generous cab-ride slush fund in the morning.

We see each other quite a bit that winter and seem to really like one another. I wear his sweater on chilly lonely nights in my apartment, wondering if his ex-wife ever wore his "favorite sweater," walking around with nothing else on. Whenever I give him this visual of me in his Pringle sweater, lying in bed naked underneath, it makes for a good starting-off point for phone sex.

A month or so later, he proves to like me enough to fly me down to San Francisco on Valentine's Day while he's on business there. He books me an early-morning flight for the next day while we are talking on the phone. A few hours later and a little sleep-deprived, I cab it to PDX and am off. When I arrive at the San Francisco Westin, he's in a meeting and the concierge says our room isn't ready yet because my partner upgraded to the penthouse. I only have a purse stuffed with a party dress and lingerie and happily go out to explore the city.

Around 4 p.m., we meet in the room. I'd just stepped out of the shower, he walks in, and we have one of those moments. The kiss is unreal, we are naked within seconds, and I want him so badly as I push him onto the bed and climb on top of him. We laugh, then agree to wait until later to fuck. He is so happy to see me, says we have this connection, and is overjoyed that I came down on a whim to visit him. We agree to meet at 10:30 that night after his business dinner. He leaves me some cash to have fun with until he can take me out later.

As I spend Valentine's evening in an expensive hotel bar, waiting for him for hours, a friendly stranger buys me drinks. I tell him why I'm here. This very good-looking gentleman says, "I had a 'you' once, a 'Jess,' but I ended up back with the mother of my children... just so you won't be surprised if that happens. But seriously, you're gorgeous and smart and can handle whiskey. Give this guy hell when he comes back tonight."

We drink together as we watch CNN footage of Whitney Houston's death, which had apparently happened earlier that week. Dr. Drew comes on the bar's flat screens and my new friend tells me he went to school with him at Amherst College (five miles from where I grew up) and shows me the doctor's number on his cell. After a few Jamesons, I'm convinced we should call him. I am awfully tempted to leave a voice mail for Dr. Drew Pinsky, seeking advice about my man issues that night, from the Ducca bar in the San Francisco Westin. I even convinced myself I'd be right at the top of his priority list.

My friend Westin won't be showing up any time soon, but he keeps texting me. Last call comes and goes, and the bar closes. I take the elevator with my new friend who just paid our entire night's bill and is probably wondering why he's staying on a lower floor while I'm going up to the 31st. Or why he isn't the one getting the opportunity to be with me tonight. We hug goodbye and he says to me again, "Seriously, you're amazing. Give this guy hell. Maybe lunch tomorrow?" I'm considering it.

Westin comes in shortly after, we get into bed, and he tells me how he stayed out until 2 a.m. with business partners taking tequila shots, and how it's all part of the job. I get it, but I flew to San Francisco for him on a few hours notice when he invited me for Valentine's Day (not that I care much about the holiday; I just think of it as a precursor to St. Patrick's Day), but the whole thing is a little disconcerting.

Around 5 a.m. we're talked out on everything from that night to how we feel about each other, his situation back home, how I think I never want to get married, me never wanting kids, his kids, how his ex-wife/friend doesn't know about me, their non-existent sex life, our very existent sex life, Portland, San Fran, this trip, us.

He sweetly asks if he can help me get out of my glittery gold party dress and then gets on top of me, and we fuck. The way he handles me is gentle and rough all at the same time, and it's good. Then we both pass out.

The next morning he's off to more business meetings and I awake to another slush fund, a beautiful view of San Francisco, and positive thoughts about the rest of the trip. Alone and happy, I gallivant throughout the city. I take a boat tour around Alcatraz and under the Golden Gate Bridge, relax in a sushi/sake lounge for lunch, partake in some shopping, chill on a park bench, get drinks at Fog Harbor on Pier 39 overlooking the water, and walk until I almost drop. Finally, when my four-inch stilettos can't take it anymore, I hail a pedicab for the ride back to the Westin, stopping at Cask so I can buy some whiskey for the room. I love a breezy, sunny city in February. It is such a nice escape from the constant cold gray rain in Portland I have come to accept as my new climate.

I'm thinking Westin might have a break and time to play before another dinner meeting that evening. Wearing only my fluffy towel, I am on the bed, hair wet, sipping whiskey, watching MSNBC, and he comes in and is quite sick, sweating, not looking good at all. He immediately goes into the bathroom and starts throwing up, and says he thinks he needs to fly home to Southern California.

I don't know what to say. I ask if it's me, wondering if all my questions the night before were too much. He assures me otherwise. I have an overwhelming yet unnecessary feeling of Jewish guilt. He tells me how sweet he thinks I am, how beautiful I am, and how he doesn't know anyone else who would fly to a random city they'd never been to on a whim and just explore for days on end, alone, waiting for him. He keeps saying he doesn't want to be sick in front of me, and when I say I want to take care of him, he doesn't want that either. I give him the trolley-car souvenir I bought for him at Fisherman's Wharf, and we say a gloomy, confused goodbye. I'm pretty sure this man will never see me naked or in a party dress again. He tells me he paid for one more night and insists I stay to enjoy it.

I take the little bottle of Jameson I got at the store and the almonds I bought, which are now dinner, into our luxurious bed and call my new best friend in Portland, my Special Friend, feeling like the loneliest person on earth in this most ridiculously beautiful place.

My meltdown phone call is prefaced with, "Please don't hate me; this is the biggest first-world problem ever." He says he loves me and tells me to walk over to the huge floor-to-ceiling window and take in the San Francisco skyline, all lit up at night. It looks magical, and for another night on Westin's dime, I stay here, talking to the Special Friend with a slush fund on my dresser, which I'll use to get home, and then some.

Early the next morning I take a town car to San Francisco International as my last luxury indulgence. I have a sexy Sayid Jarrah-like Iraqi driver, who used to be a translator for the U.S. military. He doesn't even charge me because he's so amused by my entertaining stories of the last few days. And that's really the beginning of the end of this whole twisted fairy tale. I can't get a flight to save my life since I'm flying standby, so I spend 12 hours in godforsaken SFO.

I do meet a 6' 8" gentleman a few years older than me at the first bar. He is on business, away from his pregnant wife. He shows me pictures of her and is so genuinely happy to be in love and expecting a child. He gives lectures across the country to college students on the dangers of drinking. His company is hugely successful, making these anti-drinking campaigns and promoting them. He later pays for our several double Jamesons, saying he can expense them. Huh?

I also meet an awesome rock-star lesbian who's in San Francisco for a rally against a church lawsuit on gay rights. Her partner is the head of a much more progressive church back in their hometown in North Carolina. She tells me they have two daughters, two hybrid cars, two cats, and she buys me tequila shots. Her toast goes something like, "Fuck them if they say we can't live our life!" Rock on! But there is only so much you can drink in airport bars, and only so many decent people to talk to in them. After a while, they all have scheduled flights to catch.

The airport starts to get rough. There are only so many newspapers to buy and read in one day. There are also the very unhappy gate agents who feel they can be bitchy to me since I'm flying standby. And then there are only a few bars I didn't find during the first eight hours, and they don't serve Jameson, only Bushmills. I have to draw the line.

I make a few frantic phone calls to my parentals and some friends in Massachusetts. They seem so far away. And then I just wait for my plane. These first few months, living on the West Coast on my own, have been full of surprises, and nothing has been easy. I am returning to the dreaded Kearney Curse apartment that I'm desperately trying to get out of, with the most disrespectful human beings I have ever known co-habitating with me. On the horizon are some job interviews but nothing particularly promising. I'm on my way back to a place where a lot of people have already let me down in terms of character, trust, and friendship. It's almost tempting to seriously consider a flight back to the East Coast, but I don't.

I suck up the tears, think about the truly great friends I have made, the adventures I have already embarked on, the hilarity of the whole situation, and I breathe. The televisions showing Woody Allen and Dick Van Dyke help as I pass from one airport terminal to another, as do the Bob Dylan and Tom Waits tunes on my iPod. I finally catch the last flight back to PDX at 12:50 a.m.

Westin texts to make sure I'm okay—in the airport and later when I get home around 3 a.m. (after I'm pretty sure a Russian cabbie ripped me off and wanted to whack me when I confront him on his overcharging me for the late-night fare). I text back that I am okay, though just barely. After entering the Kearney Curse, I see the despicable housemate couple and their poor dog that's left disgusting messes everywhere, including my bathroom. Indisputably, I've just gone from a luxurious penthouse to a squalid doghouse. Westin texts back, and he is starting to feel better. Thanks San Fran… It was real.

I honestly don't remember if Westin and I had one more encounter back in Portland after that tryst. We texted a few times, but his business deal here eventually fell through. I am grateful for the times we had, for sparing me from some Kearney Curse days and nights, and for those slush funds while I was still unemployed the first couple months. I really did like him but maybe the Ducca bar friend was right, and he went back to the mother of his children. It doesn't really matter.

Strangely enough, eight months later I'm lying in my own modest bed in a much nicer place, Pad. I'm naked with a new man, trying to catch my breath and sweating. It's August, it's hot, and the sun is pouring onto us through my bedroom window. The sex is insane, and I want it again so I start kissing his chest and neck. He makes this sexy growly noise and smiles; he's definitely ready again. This man is an animal. As I crawl on top of him and look into his piercing blue eyes, something clicks. It occurs to me that I'd seen him before meeting him just a month earlier.

I flash back to one of my first nights with Westin, suddenly realizing this man—ready to have his way with me again in bed—is the very same bartender from the Irish pub, the one who was eye-fucking me to pieces as I waited for Westin. He is the one who poured our top-shelf Scotch that chilly January evening. He soon will be known as the Mister.

CHAPTER 5

THE GODFATHER

"Do you want to be exclusive?"
—The Godfather

I meet the Godfather while frantically looking for a new place to live, with things getting unbearable at the Kearney Curse. Originally, Nomads was thinking she would live with her boyfriend so I was looking on my own. The Godfather's Craigslist ad looking for a female roommate is sprinkled with good-natured charm and asking those interested to "include a picture of your pearly whites." I respond, and we hit it off right away.

He wants to "interview" me for the position, so we meet up for drinks. After a couple bars and some inexplicable chemistry, we kiss. He makes me laugh, introduces me to some of his friends, and has intense dark-brown eyes. After that night, we are inseparable for the next few weeks. He picks me up to hang out every day, and I sense that with a budding dating scenario, moving in with him might not be the best idea. But I'd at least have a place to crash a few nights a week. And a new friend.

We have plenty of comical times together, and my Special Friend says he approves. We start to call him the Godfather because he has an aura about him, like he knows and controls the people and things around him. He has a magnetic personality, and men and women flock to him.

His energy is strong, positive, attractive, and clearly the reason I was drawn to him in the first place. The Special Friend and I joke that he runs his house like a Godfather would, with strict rules for housemates. Though *he* does whatever he wants.

The Godfather is the first vegan I ever have the pleasure of sleeping with. He's from South America and has a sweet smile, but he's not my type physically. He is short and has very little hair, reasons the chemistry that sparked between us is so surprising to me.

He seems to fall for me quickly, something he isn't particularly comfortable with. He makes plans without me a couple times to have a boys' night, but always ends up calling me later, saying he wants me to join in. Though I like him, I soon discover things that make me think he's probably not someone I could seriously date.

He has sleazy *Maxim* posters hanging in his bathroom and loves to brag about visits to strip clubs. Two highly unappealing qualities in a man his age, or any age for that matter. One day in his bedroom, he whips out a weird folder from years ago that he assembled with smutty *FHM* fold-out posters. I could never consider someone like this boyfriend material. This guy's over 30, not 14 for fuck's sake!

He attends Portland State University and has a legal medical marijuana career on the side (like so many people in this city). He also works at Portland Timbers soccer games pouring beer at Jeld-Wen Field. Soccer has become hugely popular here, and he makes good money with his side jobs while paying for school. He complains about classes, but I encourage him to try harder. To his credit, he takes me seriously. He lives in the Southeast Hawthorne area and eagerly shows me around this fun and exciting quadrant of Portland.

One of the first Saturdays after we have a sleepover, he takes me to Blossoming Lotus, a favorite spot of his. They serve hip and delicious vegan fare, with one of the best brunches I've had on the West Coast. I'm ordering my greyhound, he's on his phone, and the next thing I know he tells me his mother is going to join us. I still have on my clothes and makeup from the night before, but he insists he wants me to meet her and tells me to just be myself. He has no clue how mortified I am, but it doesn't matter. I am going to meet his mother, like it or not.

He is spontaneous, but not always in the best way unless it's on his terms. Other people's feelings don't really matter if he has his mind made up. Still, I convince myself he is actually really into me because he wants me to meet his mother, even on a whim.

I could tell by the look on her face when she walks in that I could have had a trash bag on, and she'd be happy. Clearly this man I'm so perplexed about doesn't often introduce his mother to a woman he is sleeping with, and she is quite pleased to meet me.

We have a lovely brunch and then she asks if we will be joining her for church. I've never been to church, and it's probably the last place I'd think of going on a Sunday Funday morning. But I willingly agree to see what it's all about, and the Godfather clearly wants to go. Church with the Godfather and his mother... interesting. This is something I didn't expect.

He knows a few people at this church, mostly from Portland State, and he introduces me to them all. I try to keep up reading the prayers in the Bible in front of me and get into the music. The choir is good, and I like some of the speeches. There's a bit too much Jesus this and Jesus that for my taste, but the Godfather and his mother are definitely into it.

We have a moment while sitting down, as a member of the church recites a story at the podium. The Godfather is holding my hand, being sweet and whispering things in my ear, and then he stares down at my breasts in my dress from the night before. Just as the man up front is thanking God during the turbulent tale he is sharing, the Godfather subtly smiles at me, nudges against my breasts, and says, "Thank God for those!" It makes me laugh, and I realize how bizarre this place can be.

Later that day, I ask him about his views on the whole religion thing as we have a drink on his couch, smoke a joint, and watch *Family Guy*. He says, "I'm a believer." I have no idea what that means coming from him, but quickly he reminds me how much he enjoys fucking without condoms, acting macho around women, and doing drugs. He's a believer in some things for sure.

He consistently tells me how much he is not a "relationship man," and I accept this for what it is. He's someone I could never find myself trusting in a relationship with anything more than what we have. Knowing this from the start, I accept him for who he really is, a good-natured friend. I think that's what made him fall for me: I treated him differently than the other women he was used to wanting to get into bed with. I never expected more. I was still occasionally seeing Westin, the wealthy lawyer from California, which made him sense competition. He pretended not to care but showed twinges of jealousy and thrived on it to try and win me over.

When I was in the Portland airport leaving for my trip to San Francisco to see Westin, the Godfather calls me to wish me a Happy Valentine's Day. He asks what I am doing, and I tell him the truth. He says he doesn't believe in the holiday and hopes I have a good time. I thank him, and when I return to Portland, he's more attentive than before.

He has a big black Lab named Osa who is very well-behaved. I always thought the way he treated her was how he felt entitled to treat women. He has a way of feeling that he can say commands and get people to obey, like he does with his pooch. I sense that he feels entitled to such power, but I don't buy it. I could tell by his reactions that not many women he'd slept with had stood up to him before. And he appreciated that I did.

He's generous, opening his home to me, treating me to nice meals, and being protective of me in Portland. It's a welcome change from many of the people I'd met here so far, especially the men. He is passionate about enjoying life, and he's comfortably fun to be around. We'd watch *South Park* for hours and contagiously, uncontrollably laugh with each other. And then there's the sex. It's hot. But he feels entitled as a man for certain things, like regular blowjobs and not having sex while I am on my period. This bothers me quite a bit.

One morning he wakes me by putting his balls in my mouth, for a good-morning blowjob. I find it sort of funny to open my eyes to someone in this way and go along with the whole thing while thinking *what is he fucking doing?* He is complicated in his Colombian macho ways, but he makes me laugh, is sweet to me, and I find him endearing, balls and all.

I enjoy grocery shopping with him and all our joking around about Vegenaise, Field Roast loaves, and other vegan treats. It's refreshing to be with someone with a mindset intent on not eating animals, and it feels sexy to be with someone whose values are consistent with mine on something unconventional. The awesome Los Gorditos Mexican food truck down the street from his house knows us well from our hungover mornings. Their vegan burritos with soy curls and rice, beans, and guacamole became lifesavers when our heads hurt too much to cook, and it's raining too hard to venture far.

He sings ridiculous songs for karaoke at the Hawthorne Theatre and blows the crowds away with Bon Jovi and Lynyrd Skynyrd covers. He is perpetually up for a good time. One night we split an oversize weed-laced vegan peanut butter cup (so very Portland) and go see the film *Shame.*

I should have had one bite, not half the fucking thing. I get so high I think my head is bumping into the ceiling throughout the movie. He chuckles but is very attentive, making sure I am alright. I'm not. He offers to take me out of the theater for some fresh air and to buy us a pitcher of beer. Laurelhurst Theater and many of the other modern cinemas and independent theaters around the city pride themselves on being pubs as well as places to see cheap or classic movies. I survive that night, though just barely.

The last time I was that high was on summer break from college with a few boys from home, shotgunning every hit and drinking expensive European vodka one of them stole from his parents. I swore my mom, with her awesome Jewfro hair, was Mrs. Frizzle from *The Magic School Bus* when she picked me up. To this day, I claim I had a lengthy conversation with God through the noisy air conditioning vents of her

Ford Windstar before puking on my parents' driveway. (It was one of the few times I lost that infamous bet with my father.)

That caper in the movie theater, attempting to watch *Shame*, becomes known as the "peanut butter cup incident," and it's right up there with the Frizzle buzz. Those two experiences taught me what being high really is, literally feeling like you're floating so far off the ground you can't come down. I'll be happy never to experience that again.

Speaking of Mrs. Frizzle, my mom comes to town as I'm about to move out of the Kearney Curse, and we stay at the Godfather's house some of the nights she is here. She and he hit it off. He treats her kindly, introduces her to his mom one night, takes us to brunch at Blossoming Lotus, and even throws a party at his house so she can meet some of our friends.

But then something happens in disappointing Portland fashion. There is a sudden downfall, harder than I possibly could've anticipated, when things are going so well. It starts off early in the evening when my mom, my former roommate Scout, and I go to dinner at Portobello, my favorite upscale vegan eatery in the city. I invite the Godfather, but he has a school function and says he'll plan to meet us there for dessert.

When he finally shows up, he is obliterated and with a housemate. The Godfather is rude to the server about the wine list, and he's embarrassing and obnoxious. Scout tells me of her dislike for him as soon as she meets him. I try to explain that I've never seen him like this and I'm appalled.

After finishing up, he insists we swing by Goodfoot, a quirky and intimate Southeast Portland bar he likes, with its changing art exhibits upstairs and live music in the basement. Right there in the bar, he blurts out that he wants to be exclusive with me, a conversation that feels a little inappropriate at the time as we are around others, including my mom. And he *is* quite intoxicated. I've always been understanding of him, but this was out of the blue, and I couldn't trust what his inebriated self was getting at. I reply with, "I think what we have is going good." I know in my heart that he can't be exclusive. It isn't in his genetic makeup and isn't something he ever wanted before. I'm not about to be his first experiment.

After Goodfoot we head to his house, lots of people are there, and everyone's having a good time. Later in his kitchen, I could see in his eyes how badly he wished he hadn't said what he did at the bar, and how much he resented what I had said in return. Still, I'm trying to enjoy myself and socialize. Everyone's laughing and having a blast, especially my mom. I am high, eating soy ice cream from the carton, and laughing over the ridiculous oversize neon bendy straws we're using to drink our cocktails.

I think the Godfather and I are okay. And suddenly he fucking snaps. When I try to give him a bite of ice cream, he yanks the spoon out of my hand and chucks it as hard as he can across the room. He then proceeds to rip the carton from my hands, slamming it as hard as he can into the trash.

All the people in the kitchen around us go

silent, and the whole room's air is suddenly uncomfortable and awkward. I am stunned. Friends excuse themselves from the room, and he cannot explain himself. His unnecessary and shockingly illogical drunk-ass behavior shook me, and I call him on it. He doesn't care. He yells at me about nothing in particular, and his belligerence makes me so upset I begin to cry. He marches into his bedroom and slams the door. I try to reason with him, but it's pointless. He acts like a spoiled child in the midst of a temper tantrum.

I want to leave but due to some other unfortunate circumstances (having to do with my mom), I'm forced to stay longer than I wanted. I crawl into bed with him, hoping for a hug and an apology, while I wipe away my tears. All he does is mumble more nasty words to me as he turns away and ignores me. Not touching me or saying anything, his still-blasted self passes out. I leave with my mom a few hours later by cab when she is feeling better. This friendship, whatever we had, is starting to feel like it's not worth having anymore.

We don't talk for days, due to his lack of effort. I text and call him and receive no response. I am disappointed by the Godfather and confused about his lack of communication after the incident. With some people, there's only so far you can reach out after something happens, especially after you've been let down. His lack of consideration frustrates me, and his failure to respond to my texts and calls after his party misbehavior shows me his weak underlying character. He could have quickly apologized that night, or even the next day, but for more than a week he ignores me even though it was he who'd flipped out and fucked up. He didn't seem to care, so I stop caring too.

As it turns out, he eventually tries hard to get me back, after he finds out I am seeing someone new. It's too late. I know his efforts at this point are purely because he didn't think he'd lose me so fast. He says he's sorry again and again, shows up with lunch from Loving Hut, a vegan Chinese restaurant in Portland, and invites me to a couple concerts. I am gracious but say no. The Godfather warns me about the guy I start seeing, but I attribute it to his jealousy. Thinking about it later, I realize he was right. I'll never know if the Godfather's heart was really in the right place or if his warning was driven by envy. (This new guy will soon be known as the Soulless Fuck.)

Finally, some weeks later, I agree to let the Godfather take me out for drinks, after clearing it with the new guy I'm seeing. I felt I still needed a good explanation and thought maybe we could still be friends. We laugh and make that eye contact you only have with certain people. That hard-to-explain chemistry was only a shadow of what it had been, and definitely not enough for me to reconsider him as someone I could trust.

He says he's truly sorry, tries to make excuses, but he just could not justify his actions. And I pretty much knew his unstable and insensitive behavior would happen again. He may have admitted he acted like a coward, but he didn't sound all that convincing talking about his failure to reconnect with me after the party. It was more that he didn't want to lose me than actually feeling badly for hurting me.

While talking that day, he puts his hand on my arm and we have fun taking silly photos in the bar's photo booth and playing old arcade games. We laugh a little, but not like we used to. He brings me to Food Fight, the vegan grocery store, and insists we keep hanging out that night.

But I tell him to please bring me home, and he does. Inside Pad, he hugs me for a while, then I pull away and tell him he should go. The new guy I'm seeing is coming over. I am appreciative that he trusts me to see the Godfather today, and he knows that I wouldn't do anything to mess up what we've started.

The Godfather gives me a look, and he's kind of sad. I can see it in his big brown Colombian eyes, but he says he's glad we got back together for the day. I tell him I am too. Although I sense that we'll probably not see each other again.

As he leaves, he stops and asks if he can show me something. I say yes, and he then shows me a quote in his phone, from Dr. Suess. He tells me that he saw it in school the other day and thought of me. It reads, "We are all a little weird and life's a little weird, and when we find someone whose weirdness is compatible with ours, we join up with them and fall in mutual weirdness and call it love."

I smile, tell him I like it, and say goodbye to the Godfather.

CHAPTER 6

THE SOULLESS FUCK

"You're the most beautiful woman and the best girlfriend I ever had. You are an angel."
—The Soulless Fuck

After the Godfather's meltdown, I am feeling pretty bummed. Moving into Pad, I keep thinking about how things ended, and about this bizarre Portland scenario I find myself in. One night, a couple of new friends convince me to go with them to the Hawthorne Theatre. They assure me the Godfather won't be there. By now I should have detached myself from all things Godfather-related. Still, I'm pretty sure I can trust these two, with whom I've become quite close, though they are his housemates. Turns out they are more trouble than they're worth, but that night I remain optimistic, pull myself together, wear a Bob Dylan T-shirt, a cute hat, tight leggings, and am determined to have a good time. The last thing I'm expecting is to meet someone new.

I meet the Soulless Fuck for the first time that night. He's sitting on one of the benches by the windows at the bar, wearing a goofy Jamaican hat. He has a great head of crazy curly hair and nice eyes. He's tall, fit, and very funny. The Godfather's housemates insist on what a good guy he is, as they've all known each other for quite some time. I ask him if he wants to switch hats, and he agrees.

We hang out at the Hawthorne Theatre with our mutual friends and then spend this first night together breaking into a hot tub in a nearby apartment complex after drinking at the bar. We get naked and hook up but don't fuck there, even though the chemistry is intense. While getting dressed after the hot tub, we get silly and put on each other's clothes before entering the 24-hour Hotcake House for a midnight snack. The men behind the counter want to kill Soulless for walking in with my soaking wet and skin-tight leggings, his entire package bulging out. We don't care. We're high on life and will stay that way for much of the next few months.

We spend the next few days gallivanting around Southeast Portland, admiring the ducks in Laurelhurst Park, eating delicious Lebanese food on Hawthorne, and having sleepovers every night in Pad. I'm happy to be comfortably settled in here, and things are looking up.

After three days of being together non-stop, I

receive a call from the recruiter I've been using to help find work, and I'm offered the job I will end up taking. I remember that morning well. A little hungover from the long night before, I throw on a black suit and cab it to this downtown office. (Coincidentally, it's just across the way from my friend Olympic's apartment.) This company will go through many changes with ownership through my next year and a half there, but it turns out to be the best job I probably could have here. It puts my people skills and business knowledge to good use. Though some managers are difficult at first, the hardest part is waking up at 6:30 every morning and walking the two-plus miles downtown across the Hawthorne Bridge in heels, rain (more often than not) or shine.

But it's as if my dark Portland cloud has lifted. After these first three challenging months, suddenly in one week everything seems to fall into place. I have an ideal apartment with an amazing roommate, Nomads, a new man, and a job. *Finally!*

Soulless and I meet daily for lunch at the food carts behind my office when Homegrown Smoker, the vegan BBQ food cart, has a location there, and he rides his bike downtown to meet me at 5:00 after most workdays. He works less than part-time at some lame chain restaurant serving food and beer, and he attempts a medical marijuana career on the side. Just knowing that, I should have realized what a loser he was right then and there. This guy is a good five years older than me, but I am an equal-opportunity benefit-of-the-doubt kind of person, and we seem to connect.

He is German, Jewish, and Irish. He spent time in Germany growing up, as my father did, and he seems to have a good head on his shoulders. He appears to be smart, well-traveled, and makes me laugh. He knows Portland well, and I like his sister. His hobbies include dodgeball and lots of outdoor activities. I become a regular at his dodgeball games every week and that opens up another social circle for me, albeit an odd one. It's fun nonetheless. And so very Portland.

He basically moves into Pad shortly after we start dating. I think we spend three nights apart in the four months we are together. He'd been temporarily living at his grandfather's house in far-out Southeast Portland. The last real place he called home was a house with an ex-girlfriend, but she cheated on him and he split. I happily consent to letting him stay with me, and Nomads approves.

He is grateful enough, though discourteous at times when it comes to acknowledging the fact that I have a roommate. This is a problem one night when he can't keep his voice down, watching mindless YouTube videos and bellowing on about one of his lame conspiracy theories. He's into believing everyone is against freedom and how 9/11 was a massive government plot that somehow didn't really happen. He never wanted to believe in "the system" as he called it, in corporations, or even working for a living. I come to realize he is the opposite of ambitious, but at the time I mistake it for being spontaneous. I almost kick him out right then and there during this loud, rowdy night. I promise Nomads it will never happen again. He is apologetic, but there will be future outbursts.

Mixed Martial Arts (MMA) becomes another hobby of his, and he takes it seriously. I don't understand why he is wasting his time and money on it, and it only seems to make him scarily intense and aggressive in unpredictable ways. I find his outbursts, like the one in Pad, come from that MMA mentality and drinking too much. He is working only about 20 hours a week and constantly complaining about his lack of funds and job. Slowly, I start to see the effects of his daily weed smoking. I let it slide, thinking I'm in love.

The first time I say "I love you," we're lying in bed and I tell him I have something I want to say. He responds, "You *know* that I am in love with you too, right?" I did, but never quite understood why I had to say it first. He says he fell in love with me the very first day we hung out, sitting outside TarBoush, a Lebanese restaurant, having cocktails and lunch. It was only a few hours after we'd met, the night before. He claims he couldn't say it then because it happened so quickly. I guess this makes sense.

He repeatedly tells me how I saved him. He explains how depressed he was after his ex cheated on him, and he was miserable. He says I changed his life and calls me his angel.

Most of the time he's quite affable, and we explore bars all around Portland. We are both into good craft beers, enjoy watching silly movies together like *There's Something About Mary,* and just laughing with one another. I cook dinners for him because he loves the vegan food I introduce him to, and we text constantly when apart from each other.

Physically, I am totally attracted to him, with his luscious curly hair, chiseled features, and trim body. People like to comment on the fact he looks like Jesus. He is taken by surprise at how attentive and sweet I am to him, but he seems to appreciate it. From time to time, he says how he thinks I am too good for this world. I come to care for him deeply, and he acts like he feels the same way.

We soon have our fun routines, like going to Hungry Tiger Too on Wednesdays for vegan corn dog night, and venturing to Laurelhurst Theater for cheap movie nights. He shows me how to get around the city by foot, as neither of us have a car, and that really helps me get my bearings here.

On St. Patrick's Day, I tell him I want to go all out. Having lived in Dublin, I love this holiday's festivities. He tells me a buddy is having a party outside of town, but I want to stay close and go downtown with the Special Friend, to celebrate Portland-style. Soulless and I agree to meet afterward at Pad, though I'd hoped he would come with us.

The Special Friend and I end up partying the night away in a sprawling outdoor tent connected to Paddy's, a crazy Irish Pub, rocking out to the bands and meeting ridiculously clothed people. A few hours later back at Pad, a few of the friends we'd met up with come by. Meanwhile I hold the

Special Friend's hair as he gets sick in my toilet. He'd outdone himself, drinking too much Jameson and beer, and I'm happy to take care of him. Later, people are passed out on my stairs, couch, and floor, and I am in bed waiting for Soulless to come home. I awake the next morning to a half-dozen vegan Voodoo doughnuts on my pillow. Soulless bought them for me the night before. I appreciate the sweet things he does for me, and the Special Friend is grateful for this morning hangover-helper treat.

Soulless and I go see Augusten Burroughs speak one evening at Powell's Books. It's my fourth time seeing this inspiring author, and Soulless tells me how he relates to this guy in some way because of their parentless upbringings and weird childhoods. It's sad to hear Soulless talk about how he basically raised himself as a young kid. He explains how he never had anyone to pick him up from elementary school or encourage him to really care about graduating high school. I want to introduce him to my family, my world, and have him see what it's like to have a loving support system. He wants this too, very badly he says, and is excited about the prospect. He decides to book a flight to Massachusetts in the summer when I go home for my first visit since moving out west.

But our relationship is far from perfect. In the bedroom he's an amateur. I am never quite satisfied, and when he comes he screams like a crazed animal. Not sexy growly "I need you" noises, but like he's a fucking wild man. I get used to it, but it grosses me out to think about now. He comes so hard everywhere like an 18-year-old frat boy, and at the time I just sort of take it as a compliment. I realize later that he was just totally sexually inexperienced.

One day at work I am dirty-texting him during my lunch break. He's hanging at Pad, worked-up over my words, and when he goes silent I wonder what's going on. That evening, I look on my computer's history for a movie we started, and some disgusting, skanky, "big-assed" women porno site shows up. I am somewhat speechless, somewhat wanting to laugh in his face, and somewhat insulted. I call him on it, remind him I am a size 1, and won't have a fat ass or be a disgusting skank anytime soon. He's embarrassed as he should be, using *my* laptop, doing it in *my* apartment, and to *my* dirty texts to him while at work. Vomit.

On the sideline at one of the Soulless Fuck's dodgeball games, I get smacked in the nose with the ball and have to leave because I'm bleeding. He knows I am gone yet doesn't seem to care where I am after the game. This is perplexing and out of character for him considering how tight we've become. As he proceeds to get drunk at the nearest bar with his teammates, I walk home across the city hoping he'll call me. But he doesn't check in to see if I'm okay or where I am. I end up at a bar across town, alone, and ultimately cab it home. Surprisingly, he doesn't call me back or come home. This is the first of our three nights apart, and the first telling sign that he is truly a clueless, selfish fuck.

His ex never seems to be an issue, but she

texts him occasionally and he is always honest about it. I assume that a girl who has cheated on him, lied, and left him would not be of interest to him anymore. Especially since he has me, his angel. I recall one streetcar ride when she's flirtatiously trying to get in contact with him via text. He shows it to me, and as far as I know he ignored her.

Our summer trip to Massachusetts turns out to be quite wonderful, and I've forgiven him for the dodgeball incident after he seemed to feel genuinely bad and apologetic for his inconsiderate, drunken actions that night. We spend half the time in Northampton eating and drinking at my favorite spots including The Sierra Grille, Hotel Northampton, Zen, Tunnel Bar, Ye Ol' Watering Hole, and the Northampton Brewery. We attend a Dan Bern concert in the Berkshires at The Guthrie Center (as in Woody) with my family, then spend a few days in Boston with my extended family and friends. We enjoy my aunt and uncle's home in Arlington, my cousin's scenic rooftop off Boylston Street, and spend a night with my friend Colleen in Jamaica Plain. He is treated with open arms across Massachusetts, and my discerning cousin Shana is ready to consider him part of the family. He gets along well with everyone.

We have a Sunday Funday party on my parents' deck the day before we leave. My brother, his girlfriend, and other hometown friends join us. There's lots of music, hula hooping, drinking, weed, and food. Kids are there, too, enjoying the last of the Voodoo doughnuts from the big pink box we brought from Portland. It all seems right, and I am happy. He is impressed by how awesome everyone is and the great time we are having together.

Much later, I learn my dad bit his tongue about his feelings regarding the Soulless Fuck that Sunday. He says from talking to him, he sensed that he was lazy, lacked ambition and motivation, and could never really take care of me in the way I deserve. I wish he had told me that straight off the bat, but he didn't because he said I seemed so content. I probably wouldn't have heard him anyway.

We fly back to PDX on a red-eye, and his mother picks us up. We hang out with his mom and sister that day, and I have not yet been to sleep since our last day in New England. I have to be up for work at 6:30 the next morning. The Soulless Fuck has nothing much going on the next couple days except riding bikes and smoking with his pals.

He meets me after work that next day with one of his friends, and they're both shirtless and carefree on their bikes. I am exhausted, bombarded with new projects my first day back at the office. He couldn't care less, babbling nonsense about his day, his new September 11 conspiracy theory, and about wanting Ron Paul to be our next President. I doubt he has ever registered to vote, thank goodness. I don't understand these Portland men. The Godfather was all about Ron Paul too. They're all just so politically under-educated and cynical.

I try to change the subject, and he just wants to get to dodgeball. I am beginning to get irritated and tired of him never being a man when it comes to real life here in Portland, especially since I had just shown him so much love, and family, and things to be grateful for. But I suck it up and ride on his bike, wrapped around him, to his stupid game.

After hours of dodgeball, we go to the trashy bar near the Friendly House in Northwest Portland—where the dodgeball games are held—like we always do. The slutty bartender who only wears a top and heels, and never wears bottoms to her outfits, is behind the bar. I'm ready to leave after a few vodka sodas and have another long day ahead of me. I'm aching for a few hours of sleep. I tell the Soulless Fuck, and he goes inside to pay.

Thirty minutes later I'm still waiting, and I find him goofing off with the pantless bartender, chatting away about his ex-girlfriend. Apparently pantless slut, the Soulless Fuck, and his cheating ex all know each other from another bar where the ex and she had worked. He had failed to tell me this the many times we frequented this slimy place. *Hmmm...*

I get tired of waiting for him during this endless conversation. His dodgeball teammates are being drunken assholes, and his mindless, shirtless friend keeps telling me to wait because all the Soulless Fuck talked about all day was how much he loved our trip to Massachusetts and everyone he met there. But if he's truly serious about me, he would realize what an inconsiderate ass he is being. I wait a little longer, tell the Fuck I want to go, yet again, and finally give up and leave on my own.

He never checks in that night, and doesn't come home. Again. I fall asleep and have a nightmare that he's cheating on me. The next day he doesn't connect, and I know something's going on. He barely talks to me when I try texting and calling.

Two days later, I agree to meet him for lunch in the park near my office, like we used to. He looks like a homeless bum who got trapped in the rain for days on the street. He tells me nothing happened that night after dodgeball except he went to another bar, got really messed up, and crashed at his shirtless friend's place. I question him about everything, like if he hooked up with anyone or ended up at some strip club. Something is feeling so off to me about him not coming to me that night or the next day.

He swears he is telling the truth about ending up at his buddy's place and playing *Guitar Hero* after getting really drunk at a couple bars. He seems to feel badly enough and apologizes several times. I tell him I believe him and forgive him.

We go back to things like they used to be. He stays over the first night that week, but I don't fuck him. I feel uncomfortable and have a nagging feeling that I can't quite get over, despite his many sincere-sounding promises.

A few days later, he wants to take me to Portland City Grill. I get all dolled-up in my favorite little black dress, and he looks decently put together, finally, in a button-down shirt and clean pants, not looking shabby and homeless.

We get a booth and order martinis. It feels good and comfortable, and we chat. We're having a fine time when he spastically blurts out that he went to a bar, his ex's bar, the night he never came home. He had lied to me about this for a week. Not only hadn't he told me this part, but he fabricated a whole story about that night. About how he just went to one other bar in Northwest and then drunkenly fell off his bike riding home to his friend's place, played video games, and on and on. I realize none of this is true, and I sense he probably went off somewhere with his ex.

At Portland City Grill as he's telling me this surprising news, I remember seeing a mark on his shoulder one night that week as we were going to bed. I kissed the sore spot he told me he'd gotten from falling off his bike that drunken dodgeball night. He asked in a sighing and guilty sounding tone in bed that night, "Did you just kiss that spot?" And I said, "Yes, I want to make it better." He was silent. I realize in this moment at Portland City Grill that it's not a mark from falling off his bike at all. It had to have been a rug burn from God knows what he and his disgusting ex were doing.

I would have thrown my martini in his face at PCG as everything is racing through my head, but I am calm enough to realize I would never waste a drink that good on his soulless self. So I pound it and leave. I call a cab and head back to Pad, trying not to lose it in front of the cab driver.

Apparently the Fuck tries to come to my

apartment later that evening. But does not try hard enough. I am in the bathroom with Nomads, crying, and we never hear him knock. I'd done nothing but let him into my life, and I am really pissed at being repeatedly lied to about a girl who had totally screwed him over. Only days after I'd introduced him to my whole family back home.

Somehow I agree to meet with him after a few days, still thinking we might work this out. Or at least I can learn what really happened with the Fuck and his ex and why. This guy had shown devotion, potential, even love, day after day for nearly four months, and I wasn't sure how to just let it go. We sit on my couch for three hours one night talking while he explains that after the PCG night, he went to his ex's house after he tried to visit me at Pad. He claims nothing happened. He says they drank, talked, and he slept on her couch.

But he never picked up his cell when I tried to call him several times the day after that ill-fated PCG dinner. He says his phone died and he had no service. During our exhaustive three-hour exchange on my couch, he convinces me that after he went to his ex's house from PCG, it was just to talk to her and help him figure things out with me. He says he has no other women in his life to talk to, but I don't understand since he and his sister are close. I don't get why he'd look to his nasty ex for advice.

And I don't understand why he couldn't just stop fucking things up with us.

He says his ex and he had coffee the next morning, and then he left her place. He says there wasn't even a goodbye hug or anything. I think I am in love with him still, and willing to forgive his fucked-up actions. I want so badly to trust him. Some of my closest friends including Nomads, my Special Friend, and even one of my oldest friends from home who knew everything, encouraged me to try and work this out, forgive, and give him another chance. They all still thought there was potential, and I trusted and appreciated their support.

I get ready for bed after our long, exhausting conversation, and I wonder if he is going to stay for the night. He doesn't move off the couch as I am changing, and deep down I can't fight the feeling that he's lying about something. He looks kind of weird when I ask if he still has feelings for his ex, and though he says no, he couldn't quite look me in the eyes as he says he's not attracted to her hideous self anymore.

After these three hours of him swearing he's telling me everything there is to tell, I ask, "Is there anything else you want to tell me?" At this point, I am thinking he will grab me, kiss me, and say something like, *No, I just spent three hours telling you everything. I am sorry about it all, and I love you.* But he doesn't. Instead he says, "I didn't sleep on the couch at her place, I slept with her in her bed. And that next day, we didn't just have coffee. We drove for hours, did a hike, and then spent the day at the hot springs."

I vomit in my mouth, am beyond baffled at how he wasted these last three long hours with deception, how he wasted the whole week lying to me about everything, and how I wasted my last

73

four months. He was now officially a cheating, lying, fucking bastard who I can never forgive. He says, "I know I did the exact same thing to you that my ex did to me, and you didn't deserve it." He can't explain *why* he did it, but no explanation could justify his actions.

I have never been cheated on before, and it takes me weeks to recover. I know now he had to have cheated that very first night we were back from Massachusetts after his dodgeball game. This is the only explanation for his lies and deception. He had basically known after that night he would never get me back if I found out, and even though I'd been willing to forgive him, he never truly accepted this forgiveness. And he kept lying and making things worse. There was no forgiving that. Maybe if he had confessed the truth from the start, I might have forgiven him, but it was too late, baby.

He tries to contact me over the next few weeks via text messages, telling me I am the best girlfriend he has or ever will have. He tells me I am the most beautiful woman he has ever known, and the smartest and sweetest person he ever has been with. Clearly.

After a fancy office booze cruise on the Willamette River with my expanding company's new directors, I am happily buzzed as I first read his worthless words on my phone. And I text him back when we hit land. I am at the Marriott bar on the waterfront, and for the first time call him a Soulless Fuck. It won't be the last. The description is as accurate as can be for this sorry mess of a human.

The Special Friend retrieves some of my personal things that the Soulless Fuck still has from our trip back East, including my camera and hair dryer. I am so grateful to the Special Friend for doing this, and he explains that he would do anything for me.

He also says the Soulless Fuck almost bolted when he saw him, and that they ended their brief conversation with one of my favorite lines from *Lost*: "See you in another life, brother." The Soulless Fuck could only wish that people as good as that would be in his life, and the Special Friend is such a good friend for doing that for me, being there for me at this vulnerable time when I truly needed him.

My dad comes to visit me shortly after, and my spirits slowly start to lift. We go to Portland Brew Fest, nice restaurants in the Pearl District, vintage stores on Hawthorne, Last Thursday on Alberta, and we hang out with Nomads and the Special Friend. I am starting to get over the heartbreak.

Luckily, I never run into the Soulless Fuck after that. (Where do all these guys go?) I do see a couple of his dodgeball mates from time to time, but nothing ever comes up about him. I hear he may have moved to Hawaii, but I prefer to think he drowned himself after jumping off the Hawthorne Bridge one evening.

He once seriously said to me that he thought he was just bad at life, that he could not ever quite get the hang of it. At the time he mentioned this, I reassured him that couldn't be the case because I really was in love with him. But looking back, I realize it is probably the most truthful and accurate thing he ever said to me.

Sometime after our breakup, I recall that he was born on Leap Day, February 29, and have a realization. Though it's no excuse for his actions, it felt fitting that he behaved as immaturely and weakly as he did given the number of literal birthdays he's celebrated. In many ways, the guy truly was like an eight-year-old.

CHAPTER 7

THE SPICY ITALIAN
(A FLASHBACK)

"You are such a passionate one."
—The Spicy Italian

B ack home in Massachusetts, the Italian had been a part of my life for a long time. He was like a member of the family though we weren't related. He listened to music and drank whiskey with my dad on countless occasions, many of which I was happily included in during my semester off from college and after I graduated. He manned the barbecue at my brother's high school graduation party and turned out to be one of the strongest, most sincere, and honest men I have ever known.

He was some 20 years older than me. On summer vacations in Ogunquit, Maine, he'd put out my American Spirit menthol light cigarettes whenever parents were sighted, drink Chianti like water, argue with me about Whitey Bulger's whereabouts, jam out to classic Clarence Carter records again and again ("Too Weak to Fight" and "Slip Away" were favorites), and make authentic Italian meals with the best sauces from scratch. He was one of the people who always believed in me... and then he died.

I'll never forget the feeling I had the morning I went to work the day I knew he was going to pass away. I had gone with my parents to visit him earlier that morning; I'd told them, "We have to go today." I just knew.

When we got to the hospice where he was now living, he wasn't conscious but was there. I remember his wife frantically running around, desperately doing anything she still could for him. It was too late. I'd always believed he'd be okay, even after his diagnosis. I convinced myself that even with a brain tumor, he'd get well and we'd all laugh about it later.

At work that afternoon I have a gut-wrenching ache. I close my shop early. Not even 15 minutes after walking in the door of my parents' house, sitting with my mom on the couch, we get the phone call. I can't pick it up. The voicemail from his niece, who is my age and with whom I grew up, says, "Tonight he lost his battle with cancer. Come here as soon as you can." I don't even remember if I put on shoes, but my mom and I were out the door.

I walk into the room, and he's there, in peace. His two young sons by his side. I about lose it. I go to a common room to find another family member, we make small talk, and then he leaves. I call my brother, against my parents' wishes. They insist this isn't the time to tell him. He's at Ithaca College, studying for finals, partying, being a good college senior. I don't respect their wishes for once, and I call Michael.

He picks up, and I can tell he's at a small party. I can hear his college girlfriend in the background, and I say, "Hey Mikey, how are you?" He is good, busy, asks how I am, and then I say, "I have to tell you something, it's not good. Can I tell you now?" I half want him to say no. But he doesn't, and so I have to tell him. I will never forget the sounds of my brother starting to hysterically bawl, over my cell. I will never forget how much this makes me cry harder, and how much I wanted him next to me at this moment. I will never forget how hearing my own voice say the words out loud hit me, and sinking to the floor as Mikey sobbed in my ear. Finally, we are both out of tears, he tells me he loves me and has to go. He thanks me so much for telling him.

The Italian's wife said he must have felt ready to go, knowing that my parents and I had come to see him earlier that day. She said he was waiting to let go until we all came one last time to be with him. It was our goodbye.

I wrote a eulogy for the Italian's funeral service. I talk about how he was there for me, how I loved him, what a great husband and father he was, how much I will always admire him. After I finish my reading, I remember it was harder to walk back to my seat than anytime I'd ever been really drunk, my body totally wanting to give out.

Prior to the Italian getting the damn tumor, I had many great times with him. He was a trustworthy and hardworking man. He would do anything for his family and for the people he loved. I've been compared to him in the way that we would each bring different kinds of people together socially. The people you met through him were always respectable, genuine, and undeniably fun.

I remember going to visit Suffolk University in Boston with my dad, and we get lost, ending up in a sketchy part of town. Although my dad grew up in Lexington and went to Boston University, he didn't know this area at all. We immediately call the Italian, 100 miles away, and he knows the exact block we're on and talks us through the winding backstreets to our destination, guiding us past landmarks including bars and, I'm pretty sure, one legit whorehouse. He knew the city backward and forward, amazing considering he'd long been living in the same small farming community where I grew up. He and his wife moved there from Boston to raise their children in a safer, cleaner environment.

As it turned out, I never attended Suffolk. I graduated in 2007 from Lynn University in Boca Raton, Florida, and several years before venturing out to Portland, I moved back to Northampton. My college career had a successful ending at graduation when I received the Bachelor's Degree Award for the highest GPA in my class of 625 and was congratulated by our commencement speaker

Chris Matthews after the ceremony. The Spicy Italian was very happy for me.

Spontaneous visits from the Italian after college graduation found him, my dad, and me often getting pretty looped on whatever our theme was for the night. Sometimes it was college basketball and red wine, others it was foot-stomping music and Courvoisier; most of the time it was just sweet soul music, fun conversation, and lots of good drinks.

One particular night, I go to the kitchen to refresh everyone's glasses. The Italian comes with me. He's walking behind me, and when I turn to ask what he wants for a drink, we look at each other and have this moment. It's like we knew what each other was thinking, and it catches us both off guard. We hug, and it's loving and innocent. He tells me, in his kind way, how passionate I am. I hand him a glass and walk back into the living room with fresh drinks for me and my dad. That look in that brief moment, whatever it was, was probably more for comfort than anything else. He loved the closeness of our families.

There's another night around the same time where my dad goes off to sleep early, and the Italian and I are left alone. We'd been watching *The Dean Martin Show,* several seasons of which my dad had randomly purchased from an infomercial late one night. We also played the classic Dino 45 "Little Ole Wine Drinker Me" over and over on the stereo. The Italian and I proceed to get buzzed and talk about everything from men I date to Ireland to fuckhead George W. Bush to South Beach to veganism till all hours.

I wake up a few hours later. It's morning, and the hat I was wearing is on the floor. I'm on my parents' couch in my clothes from the day before. The Italian calls my cell. I answer and ask about last night. He said we had great fun, he had to leave to go to work very early, and just wanted to check in. My cheeks hurt from laughing so much with him.

My family and I start seeing less of him after he gets diagnosed. It was around the time I was in a serious car accident, creamed by a drunk driver one night driving to my parents' house at 2 a.m. I was coming back from a forgettable concert in Northampton, Colbie Caillat, and now every time I hear that happy and bubbly pop hit song of hers, I want to vomit. It reminds me of one of the worst nights of my life.

After this drunk-fuck driver hit me and my Oldsmobile Alero, he passed out in his car. My airbags deployed, all my things went flying onto the road, including my shattered cell, and glass is everywhere. I can't open my driver-side door because it's jammed shut from impact, but somehow I pound my way out, causing a painful bruise on my left arm. Fight or flight, I saw my car smoking and kept telling myself I wasn't going to pass out or die that night on the street, even though I could barely move.

I couldn't walk and could tell my knees and back were pretty messed up. But I crawled across the road to the other car. I start banging on his window screaming, "You just fucking hit me!" He was out cold. In this small farming town in Western Massachusetts, on the back roads at 2 o'clock in the morning, there is no one around and no cars for miles. I wait on the side of the road crying for what feels like hours. It's the third day of November and really cold. Finally two young guys and a woman attempt to drive by in their pickup truck, but can't because of the mess of car pieces and glass. They see me, and the guys scoop me up from the street, lift me into their truck, and call 911.

I never find out who these people are, as they take off when the cops and ambulances arrive. But to me, they were like angels that night. The drunk fuck got cut out of his car with the Jaws of Life, and the paramedics in my ambulance are asking me questions about what happened. I can't think straight, and my parents are hours away in upstate New York. I tell the paramedics I need to use a phone because I have to call my mom and dad. Everyone knows a 2 a.m. phone call is never good news, and my parents probably broke the speed limit many times that night after I told them what happened.

In the ambulance, I tell the paramedics I am not going to sit in the emergency room by myself. They say they can drive me home, but only if I answer some basic questions, as they weren't sure if I'd hit my head upon impact.

First, they ask what day it is. I don't know but say Friday. I'm right, and then they ask when my birthday is. I could never forget my favorite day of the year. When they ask who is the President of the United States, I say, "Someone I never would have voted for!" (It's 2007.) This makes everyone in the ambulance chuckle, and they agree to drive me home. A sweetheart cop says he'll stay with me as long as I stay awake. When my parents get home a few hours later, we go straight to the doctor.

It was all pretty miserable, but I was lucky. Lots of bruises, badly messed-up knees, and a compression fracture in my back that kept me in physical therapy for about a year. Sadly my beloved two-door silver-blue Oldsmobile Alero didn't make it, totaled after four years at college in South Florida—with weekend trips to South Beach and never so much as a speeding ticket. But shortly after graduation, I get hit less than two miles from my parents' house, the house I grew up in. I am that statistic.

During my slow recovery, I was asked to do some nude modeling for the Amherst College Art Department. After classes, those college boys (and girls) thanked me profusely for my time and yoga poses. Talk about physical therapy at its best.

The Italian learned about his cancer around the time of my car accident. One of the most remarkable and telling things about him is that even though he knew his days were numbered, when we'd talk on the phone every week or so, his first question was always about how I was doing, asking about *my* physical therapy, *my* recovery. Years later, I still choke up thinking about this. He was that considerate, that selfless.

The Italian was gorgeous inside and out. I will always think about him on holidays, on his birthday. Any time a series of toasts are being made at a family event, I raise a glass to the Italian. Since being in Portland, I think of him often. His memory always reminds me that some men are truly stand-up guys, that somewhere I will find one, and it will be someone he'd approve of. So far, none of the men I have dated here would pass the Italian's test and his high standards for me, that's for sure.

I tear up every time I hear an Earth, Wind & Fire song, as he used to tell me stories of listening to them all the time growing up in South Boston. I get shivers every time I see someone make this certain hand gesture he used to make, like *eh, whatever* while flitting his hands through the air. I think of him every time I hear an exotic-sounding Italian name come up in a story, and every time I think of what passion really is. I know he wanted me to find true love, someone who would cherish me, and I know he believed in me. I want to make the Italian proud. Cheers to you my friend.

CHAPTER 8

THE MISTER

"There's sex, there's good sex, and then there is fucking-burning-down-the-building sex."
—The Mister

The Oregon Country Fair takes place in Eugene late July each year, and it is one of the most magical and fantasy-filled lands you can experience. The music and nakedness and craziness is something I now crave like air. I want to live here year-round. Everywhere there are vegan food stands, breasts being painted, glittery wings, tutus, and tattoos. It's summertime and everyone's happy. If I ever believed in heaven, this would be it. My friend Dane, my housemate Nomads, and I have no idea what we are walking into when we arrive with open minds and vodka-filled water bottles.

We plant ourselves in the main music area for a Woody Guthrie birthday celebration at 11 a.m. on Saturday. And as much as I swoon over "This Land Is Your Land," I have to admit the tan, topless, beautiful-head-of-haired man stretching his yoga bones out right in front of me in the grass grabbed my attention.

During the next few hours, I'm having falafels, taking off clothes, drinking Pinnacle out of plastic, dancing to Beatles cover bands and reggae bands, seeing my friends getting utterly sunburned, and having an epic time. Ten hours later, during the raucous last band of the day, I see a tall, gorgeous, blue-eyed gem wearing a straw-like fedora, totally into the music. I slide up next to him in my now-wrinkled lingerie dress and bright-red high heels. He notices me immediately, compliments my shoe choice, and we dance around each other. He gives me these smoldering stares and smiles so I grab him and kiss him, not knowing what I am getting myself into. He makes this growly "I need you" sound under his breath, and I start laughing.

I tell him, "I'm so sorry, I just had a water bottle full of vodka," and he laughs a sexy, slightly older-man laugh. We switch hats so I'm wearing his fedora and he's rocking out in my oversize black sun hat. We both live in Portland and agree to meet after the festivus to get our hats back. But we're not leaving before going at it for a good 20 minutes, Nomads and Dane looking on and smiling as we make out. The way he kisses is intense and hard, his hands are all over me, and I want him so badly I consider fucking him in the corner where he has stashed his guitar, but I don't. He is staying for the whole long weekend, we are leaving that night, and I masturbate thinking about him back home in Portland.

I'm walking home from work, on the Hawthorne Bridge, when he calls me the first day back in the real world. I tell him I'll happily meet him for happy hour. He offers to pick me up, and I say "no thank you" because I love my walks around the city, and I don't quite know him yet. We plan to meet at Dig A Pony, one of the bars near Pad that I frequent in Southeast. I have that moment while walking, thinking *what if I don't recognize him?*

I walk into the bar, and I could *not* mistake this man. Striking blue eyes, about 40, perfect salt and pepper facial hair, sexy as fuck. Aviator sunglasses tucked into his neckline, the same ones he was wearing at the Oregon Country Fair before he revealed his eyes when we kissed. I slide up next to him and sit down. The first thing he says is how he just watched me walking with my hot pink dress and heels as he drove by. Apparently, he could not mistake me either. We start talking, and it turns out he's from Long Island, knows Northampton, and loves Grace Potter as much as I do. We get along famously, and I want him inside me. He is truthful from the start about his kids, divorce, and his job. Honesty is the biggest turn on for me.

Turns out he's a bartender/manager/musician at my favorite pub downtown, where many a night

I've lost my debit card or dignity or memory and wound up with a hangover from the combination of Jameson and the Voodoo doughnuts I inevitably end up drunkenly eating right next door. We kiss, fuck around, and can't keep our hands off each other as we walk out of Dig A Pony. Then he drops me off at Pad because he has to go to his kids. Fucking kids...

Over the next several months we fuck a lot. He and I can never once get through my doorway without him having his way with me on my stairs, and I love it. He will knock, and as soon as I come down I am thrown against the wall hard, kissed hard, forced down on him, then he goes down on me. And then picked up and somehow flat out naked on my stairs, fucked there, then in the living room bent over my couch, on my wood floor, on my deck, and we eventually make it to my bed where the same things happen again. He loves to smack me around as much as I love him to do it to me. He writes me lengthy sexts daily describing all the crazy things he wants to do to me, and I think about them and am willing. He's like my very own sexual version of that phony Mister Grey character, but better and real.

We have a serious conversation in the shower one time when he says we had the perfect moment at that magical Oregon Country Fair, meeting each other, making out, then realizing we both live in Portland. While we wash each other, he talks about how the ex who broke his heart was my age, and how he needs to get serious with someone closer to his age and isn't ready for anything girlfriend-wise. I tell him I'm totally over my soulless-fuck of an ex who broke my heart here in Portland, that I don't think I want a boyfriend, and that I can be a little handful sometimes. He laughs, knowing this to be the case, and kisses me.

He asks what I think of him, and I honestly answer that I don't see him as boyfriend material, but he's definitely one of the best fucks I've ever had. I then ask what he thinks of me, honestly. He makes this dangerous laughing sound as he looks at me with his piercing blue eyes, and says being with me is fucking unbelievable, unlike anything else, and what we have sexually is earth shattering. He says, "There's sex, there's good sex, and then there is fucking-burning-down-the-building sex." He shudders and smiles at me.

We're clearly so content with the answers we hear that we fuck in the shower, then back in my bed again. Breathless and lying with our heads on the foot-end of my bed, we talk about Wilco and My Morning Jacket and the Green River Festival back in Massachusetts. Before I know it he has to go pick up his kids.

During these months, I see him often at his bar and we keep up communication about what we're up to, via text. One night he promises to come over after his shift at 2 a.m., but doesn't show. Over the phone, he gives some bizarre excuse the next day and we get into a squabble about the whole thing as I am about to go rafting down the Clackamas River with the ever-reliable Olympic and some friends. Out of the blue, the Mister says he doesn't think we should talk anymore because he hates the drama of arguing. I tell him how idiotic that is after all the good times we have had, and almost throw my phone in the water, but don't. The next day he calls and admits he didn't mean what he said, and that I was right. It's like we've actually developed a friendship on top of the sex. He becomes a go-to person in Portland for me and not just for an insanely good fuck.

I call him one cold drizzly morning, still buzzed at 6:30 a.m. after my Special Friend leaves Pad, where we wound up after celebrating my one-year Portland anniversary the night before. That night had been full of adventure, including me missing texts from the Mister wondering where he can meet me after his gig downtown.

At the time, my Special Friend and I were in the process of getting interrogated by alcohol monitors in the basement of another downtown nightclub. I fell over a bar in the club, probably trying to order us shots, as my Special Friend tried to call a cab with my blush compact, thinking it's my iPhone. Messes that we are, we're put in a pedicab by security to avoid cops, and we somehow make it safely back to Pad. I don't see the Mister's texts until early the next morning. The only true way to celebrate a Portland anniversary, apparently, is to regress to the way you would have behaved the previous year. Or worse.

The Mister shows up 10 minutes after I call him back that next morning, and something is different in the way he fucks me. He can, then he can't. This has never happened, and he says he needs a short nap because it's too early. I don't

91

believe him, and then he tells me the truth. Turns out he is seeing someone. He's trying to see someone older, he "can't keep fucking 28-year-olds," and he's "sorry."

He realized how much he wanted to see me, but being with me feels like cheating. What he doesn't seem to get is he actually *is* cheating. He is genuinely apologetic and tells me he's always wanted to be completely honest with me because he remembered that's what I always told him I liked about him, besides the sex. We say a somewhat lengthy goodbye, he tells me he will see me again someday, and naked.

I crawl back under my covers and finally fall asleep. When I wake up a couple hours later, I feel like the last 12 hours of partying and club basements and the Mister were a total dream. I wish he was with me at that moment in my bed, and I can barely move so I watch Pornhub and masturbate, thinking about him. I wonder why he even came over so quickly in the first place. And then I wonder if he thinks about me while he's fucking his new girlfriend, or just when he's jerking off.

We write to each other, maybe in hopes of trying to understand one another, just telling each other how much we already miss the sex. He says I turn him on so much and how he gets hard every time I text him. He says, "I fucking love having sex with you and believe me, I don't want to stop. At the same time, I want to do right by the woman I'm seeing." He says being with me is "fireworks exploding," and I tell him, "I could not live without fireworks and buildings burning down." And he says, "Me either."

He texts me out of the blue on New Year's Eve, after a break in our communication: "Hey you, I wanted to wish you a Happy New Year! Sorry we didn't get to have more Sunday Fundays toward the end of 2012. But I think that just maybe we can start enjoying them again soon. Have a great New Year's party tonight, whatever you end up doing... I have a feeling you will."

He contacts me several times after the new year begins, making me crave him badly, even more than usual just because I cannot have him. Maybe things will land us naked together again, as he keeps telling me they will, but maybe that won't happen. He's clearly made his choices. I just don't understand why he only tells the truth with me, and not his girlfriend, or even himself. I slowly let go of my attachment, and my feelings for him fade, not unlike the way his fingerprint bruises used to on my ribs, breasts, and neck.

My friend Sara once said, "With all the much-older men you date, and the way you like to get treated in bed, anyone would think you have the biggest daddy issues ever. But your dad is like your best friend. It makes no sense!" I guess I'm just complicated.

I end up seeing the Mister again at his bar when my mom visits me in town and wants to go dancing, and he's bartending. She can't stop saying how he's "very easy on the eyes." He keeps telling me how good I look, and how much he loves my white fluffy wannabe Ushanka hat I'm wearing that night. We have a thing with hats it seems.

He looks amazing as he hooks us up with hefty pours of Jameson, and his subtle ways keep me interested. Could that be why I lose my passport to the Portland party gods later that evening and form a Radio City-style kick-line on the street in front of Voodoo Doughnut with my friend Sara, the Special Friend, and my mom?

After that night, the Mister and I are in touch from time to time, and he's always putting in the not-so-subtle "Don't ever say never" when we talk about fucking again. He's also telling me how badly he still wants me, how much he thinks about me, yet can't have me because of his circumstances that he wants to make work. I don't know what to think, but I have a feeling it won't work out for them. I start to anticipate the weekend when my phone flashes a text from the Mister, saying, "Hey you, what are you doing? I have found myself with a free afternoon…"

A few weeks later, I do receive a text from him and it turns into a lengthy conversation about his new situation, about how much he appreciates me always being so understanding of him, and ends with him saying, "Are you home? I might be in your neighborhood."

I open the bottle of Jameson on my counter, am tempted to say no to him, almost as much as I'm tempted to ask him to swing by Voodoo Doughnut on his way over. And just like this favorite combination of mine, which I know will soon leave me with regrets, I say yes.

CHAPTER 9

THE BIRTHDAY SCARE

"I don't have a girlfriend, I promise."
—Vince

You know a city has it in for you if it attacks you the day after your birthday. My friend and co-worker Devan and I are sitting at Star Bar in Southeast Portland, chatting away about her husband, our jobs, the Soulless Fuck, the Mister, etc. It is the day after my 28th birthday, and the celebration continues. The bar is cozy and cool, and it is very hot on this July evening. She offers me a smoke, we settle up, and move to a bench outside.

Devan is new to our company and a great addition to the IT department as we are expanding and in hiring mode. She's eight years older than me and married, but loves to live life, laugh, booze, and is kind and protective of me. She and her husband are from the Portland area, and on holidays and weekends they seemed to have adopted me. We'll end up spending Thanksgiving and Christmas together this year.

On various occasions, she insists on driving me home in the pouring rain as I start my walk from our office over the Hawthorne Bridge, and she always reminds me of the first time we met. I approached her the day she started working at our company, and she was a little standoffish, but I didn't give up. I asked her to join me for happy hour after work and she couldn't go, but our friendship was kindled. The next week she took me up on the offer.

When she says she owes me a birthday drink and demands I get in her car after work, I am happy. She takes me barhopping in Southeast to some of her favorite places, and at Slow Bar things start to happen.

It's here I see one of the most gorgeous men I have ever set eyes on in Portland. He is tall, has long curly dark hair, big blue eyes, and could be a stunt double for Adrian Grenier, the way he looks in the early *Entourage* seasons. He glances at me and asks to join us at our outdoor table. I say yes and call him Vince.

We have a couple rounds and chat about Portland, about bars we hang out in, what we do for work, and start to get to know each other. More than once, I ask Vince if he has a girlfriend. He insists no. After the Soulless Fuck and the Mister, I am more cautious than ever about getting involved with someone, and sadly these days, I seem to have lost my trust in just about everyone.

Later that evening, we venture around the Southeast area and all end up at the Hawthorne Hideaway. This is a divey, dark bar with the most warped pool tables on earth and messy bathroom walls from people drawing and scribbling all over them with permanent markers. It is always fun here, and only four blocks from Pad. I have experienced strange things at the Hideaway, such as nuggets of weed tossed to me, five-finger Jameson pours, lots of really bad pool playing, and stellar falafel burgers. But I always feel comfortable. It's one of my hood bars.

When Vince says he wants to join us in our Hideaway festivities, I encourage him, but not before asking once again if he has a girlfriend. Something about him just seemed hesitant when we first kissed outside Slow Bar, and I couldn't be too sure.

Vince is with a buddy, who throughout the night is persuading me to invite some of my other girlfriends to join us so he won't feel alone. Since Devan is married, Vince's friend felt that some single girls would make a nice addition for himself. The buddy works as a manager at another familiar downtown bar, and he is definitely keen on the idea of Vince and me being together this mid-summer night.

More people join us at the Hideaway, and we end up closing the bar. I ask Vince, who can't drive because he's had a few too many, if he'd like to have a sleepover when we leave. He agrees, wholeheartedly, and when we get back to Pad we get naked and fuck around. We are tipsy, laughing, and having fun, while trying not to be too loud with Nomads asleep in the next room. We never have sex, but he comes nonetheless. I am not thinking of him in a relationship sense, more just like an exciting fling. He keeps telling me how gorgeous he thinks I am and how much he wants me. I want to have fun with him, but I have no high expectations for the future. Although I certainly wouldn't mind if it were to turn into something more than a one-night stand.

We both sleep peacefully that night, but at 7 a.m. he awakes abruptly and says he has to go. While he quickly puts on his clothes, I sit up, naked, and ask if everything is okay. He says something to the effect of having an early day. I know this guy could not have an "early day" on a Saturday to save his life because of how casual he was the night before, and he never mentioned anything about having to get up early. But I'm too tired to inquire.

Monday morning comes too soon, and while at my desk at work, I keep getting phone calls on my cell from him. Three calls in the morning, two in the afternoon. But no messages. I know that something has to be going on, but I can't pick up because I am too busy with accounting batches and work calls and figure I'll call him after work.

That night I get calls from a different number. I am out in the Pearl with my Special Friend doing our Monday Funday routine, which includes happy hour at P.F. Chang's, Powell's Books, and

Whole Foods grocery shopping. While the Special Friend is driving us back to Pad, I receive a couple more of these peculiar calls. I have a gut-wrenching feeling that it is not good news and probably has something to do with the weekend. I do not call Vince back because I know these latest weird phone calls are not from his number, but I have a sneaking suspicion that they have to do with him. I also intuitively feel that if I try to call him back on his number, he won't be the one answering his phone.

On Tuesday at work, I receive a text message from the same random number as the night before. And then comes the shocker of the week for me: apparently it's from Vince's *wife*. She texts me a whole long spiel about how she went through Vince's phone, found our conversations, and made him tell her all about our escapades over the weekend. Silly me, asking all those times if he has a girlfriend. Never once did I specifically question if he was married. Fucking men. And I couldn't believe he was out with this annoying buddy of his, encouraging us to hook up the whole time. Portland never ceases to amaze me.

The wife proceeds to text me, telling me she knows everything that happened, and that her husband has a venereal disease, herpes, and explains how I shouldn't feel guilty but should get tested. I grab Devan in the IT department at work, and she takes me outside to smoke and calm me down. She thinks the wife is probably still in a relationship with him, but lying about the STDs. I can't be too sure, and she promises to take me to Planned Parenthood right after work.

I text the wife, apologizing profusely for something I never knew, and then ask her to please stop contacting me. She obliges. I never speak to her again, and I never try to contact Vince. Most likely he would not be the one answering his phone if I tried him, and I have no reason to talk to him.

Thinking back, I don't know if they were married, but I have a strong feeling he was probably involved with her, possibly engaged. With someone who looks like he does, I am sure it's not the first time he cheated. I also think this woman is just proud to be with him and lets him get away with whatever he likes. I hate this way of thinking, but some women are just that way. After what I went through with the Soulless Fuck and the Mister, I feel this is the cherry on top for me with a string of disappointing, lying, cheating fucks in Portland. I become more untrusting in the male species in this city than I ever thought possible.

Thankfully, everything is fine with me. Spending half a day at Planned Parenthood isn't exactly my idea of a good time, but the tests all come back negative. I do feel fortunate for that but wonder why I keep getting kicked while I am down in Portland. I start to really resent the people in this city. I feel like I give honest chances to men, to people, and most of them keep fucking me over. I cannot understand it and feel the urge to give up on this town. But I don't, not yet.

One night, a week or so later my Special Friend and I go to the bar where Vince's buddy is a manager. It's partially out of curiosity but also because I want to confront him and ask questions about what happened. Why did he do what he had done, encouraging Vince to come home with me? Maybe they had some kind of wager about who could pick up someone and go home with them, and he'd resigned himself to the fact that he was losing. Maybe he would tell me that none of what the "wife" was telling me is true. As it turns out, Vince's buddy isn't working at his bar that night, and I just let the whole thing go.

My good friends here help me through this. Maybe there is a lesson to be learned, like not going home with a man I just met. But I was still celebrating my birthday and trying to give a cute guy a chance, and just having some harmless fun felt like an okay idea. Plus, our whole time together he came off as charming and decent. Devan even thought so, and she is not the most welcoming when it comes to meeting new people.

I keep getting up every morning and walking the two-plus miles to work and back to Pad. I keep partying in an upbeat manner and telling myself to rally, to still trust people. Sometimes I feel like I'm a character in a *Whac-A-Mole* game. I keep being my outgoing, positive, and social self, convincing myself I want to stay in Portland. Though at this point I'm not quite sure why.

CHAPTER 10

THE VEGAN PROM AND THE SOUTH FLORIDIAN

"You should find it in your heart to forgive me."
—The South Floridian

When I first heard about a vegan prom in Portland, I thought it was a joke, but it's not. I attended six proms in high school, so when my older thirtysomething friends in Portland told me that the vegan prom during fashionable Try Vegan PDX Week was a big deal, I was in.

Try Vegan PDX is a Portland group that hosts workshops including raw-food seminars throughout the year, and they organize dine-outs in cozy veggie restaurants. They support animal-rights causes and are a big part of Vida Vegan Con, a yearly confab held in Portland for vegan bloggers.

One week each summer, TVPDX puts on a series of interesting events, encouraging folks of all ages to learn about the group, veganism, and animal-rights. And there's the vegan prom and pub crawl on Mississippi Ave. It's a cool concept, and I have friends in the group who help plan the event.

My Special Friend and I are totally into this prom idea, and we go all out. He buys me a corsage and rents an adorably sexy tuxedo. I have my mom send me my senior-year high school prom gown and tiara. The floor-length, deep-cut dress is black with subtle sparkles and has an aggressive slit. Just right for the occasion.

As we get ready, I joke that all I want to do at *this* prom is get drunk and fuck, although looking back, that's not so different from my goals the first six times, as a teenager. We make cocktails at Pad and drink out of the festive Newbury Comics pint glasses I keep in my kitchen (an ode to Massachusetts), just like my parents let me do with a pre-prom drink or two as a special splurge back in high school. (Thankfully, those never degenerated into the drama of "Donna Martin graduates," *Beverly Hills 90210*-style.)

We go to a pre-prom party at some vegan friends' home, and there's plenty of booze and people in ridiculously awesome and weird formal attire. This year's theme has a vintage feel. I'm thinking 2002 is vintage at this point, and *aaah,* that *was* my senior year of high school. The men look handsome in their tuxedos, and I can't wait to see what's in store when we actually arrive at the event.

The friends I know, a vegan couple in whose

house we are, have been very sweet to me these past few months. They helped me look for jobs and apartments in the beginning of my Portland adventure. They've met both my parents, were extremely supportive after the Soulless Fuck incident, showed me nice vegan restaurants, and sometimes picked me up after work. We'd become quite close. Turns out they have a somewhat older guy from South Florida staying with them for the week. He's quite appealing to me, and we have much in common talking about South Beach, wine, and food. Plus he's been a vegan for a decade, just like me.

He's nearly 20 years older than me, but youthful in spirit, good-looking, and fun in a South Florida kind of way... meaning wealthy. He is tan, tall, dirty blond, fit, a typical South Beach look physically. I know a number of South Floridians—unfortunately, some too well—from five years of living in Boca Raton. For me in college, even at 18 there were always guys, many of them douche bags, arrogantly flashing their credit cards to bouncers and security outside of that week's hotspot club. Ultimately, they'd get my girlfriends and me into Mynt or Mansion in South Beach on Ocean Drive. A nice break after a week of classes and homework. Now, I can only think that this houseguest guy, this older vegan, is more mature than those credit-card flashers from yesteryear.

But I can never be too sure. The year after my commencement, I went back to Lynn University to see friends graduate, and while there I caught up with some of my favorite professors. After that 2008 graduation, I found myself celebrating at the Elbow Room, a divey Fort Lauderdale bar. I met a man there from Massachusetts. I called him Christopher as he has a daughter named Lorelei (an ode to *Gilmore Girls*). He lives in Fort Lauderdale now, is 18 years older then me, and we'd be friends for several years after that. Chris and I shared some good times in South Florida and up in Boston and Northampton, but after a handful of encounters, his misogynistic mindset slowly began to creep in. Though not obvious at first, he believes men have power over women and is convinced he will never change.

After I got to know him, I learned some of his macho beliefs, such as younger is always better, and that for him nothing is more important than getting rich. He feels entitled to women and to paying not a penny more in taxes than absolutely necessary. He used to work for Bill Clinton back in the early-'90s, and I think I would have respected Chris back then, before he became affluent, moved South, and changed his outlook on life. It took a while for me to see all the things I couldn't stand about him.

But I get the feeling this new vegan South Floridian, who's friends with my good friends here in Portland, might just be different. At this pre-prom party, my Special Friend begins to see the connection between the vegan South Floridian and me, and goes off searching for someone for himself that night. I encourage him to have some fun.

We all arrive at the prom by cab after taking

pictures and drinking some tasty red wine that the South Floridian had bought for us at Whole Foods.

At the prom there is vegan pizza, a cool deejay set-up, and a bar, and the night looks promising. Shortly after we get there, I find myself and the South Floridian with a flask, hooking up against a bathroom wall. It's a unisex bathroom, he is super aggressive, and it's kind of fun.

As the night progresses, there's lots of dancing to bad '80s music and some drinking at the bar. After it ends, my Special Friend tells me he is going to hook up with a woman he's been dancing with, and I'm happy for him. He knows I've already been with someone else, and just like in high school, there's a lot more picture-taking outside in the warm air after the prom ends. I wind up back at my friends' place, where the South Floridian is staying, and we sleep together.

He's aggressive and tells me what he wants in that entitled way that older men I meet from South Florida do. I know he only fucks women my age and that he can get away with it, just like Chris. The similarity makes me feel comfortable.

The next morning those of us who stayed in the house cook brunch, and the South Floridian says he wants to hang out with me the whole week he's in Portland. My friends are putting him up because they've known him for years, and this has long been the crash pad on his Portland vacations. He and I lay in a hammock and sunbathe topless. We drink good champagne and talk all morning. I sense him to be a decent guy.

Our mutual friends encourage us to be

together, telling me what a catch he is. I trust them, and since they've known each other such a long time, I sense I can trust him. Despite his aggressiveness in bed, he is kind, respectful, and generous to me. He pays for my cab so I can go home to change out of my prom dress and heels and then return for the day. We relax and chat about Portland, veganism, and the East Coast. We discuss our families and how important we believe they are in our lives, and we discuss sex, and how important that is to both of us, too.

Later in the day, we all head to the Alberta Street Fair. There's lots of music, craft vendors, and food trucks here in Northeast Portland. Strangely enough, I find out later that the Mister is playing with his band here, but he never sees me walking down the street, holding hands with the South Floridian.

The fair is kind of a mini daytime version of Last Thursday, the madcap music-and-food-filled extravaganza here on bustling Alberta the last Thursday evening of each month from May through September. I think if you combine the carefree froth of Northeast Portland in the summertime with the feel of Bourbon Street in New Orleans and throw in some kiddie fare, it approximates Last Thursday. There are crazy people bike jousting and fire dancing, lots of music, beer tents, food vendors, organic cotton candy, and milkshakes on a stick. There are vintage stores set up in school buses, and the streets are blocked off so the throngs can just stroll along and savor the night.

On this August afternoon, it's hot and the South Floridian is holding my hand tightly as we walk, kissing me every chance he gets. We are smiling at each other, and he is particularly sweet and endearing.

A few hours later when he and I return to our mutual friends' house, we fuck and take a nap in preparation for the vegan pub crawl after dark. I innocently ask him who he normally sleeps with and he says, "Women your age." I ask, "28?" And he nods and smiles. He goes on to talk about how he has a sex swing and tells me about other kinky things he is into in bed. I sort of think he's getting too old to be doing this kind of stuff, but who am I to judge?

We fall asleep for what feels like 10 minutes. I'm particularly exhausted, but soon get a second wind after the shut-eye, and we head to the crawl with our friends. At the first bar, the South Floridian and I are relentlessly texting each other dirty things even though we are sitting right next to each other. Eventually when everyone starts teasing us, we decide to just switch phones so we can pay more attention to our surroundings and other friends. The idea is that we won't text each other so much with the other's phone in hand. We have enjoyed each other's company all day, and even sitting next to each other it was hard not to share some intimate words.

Then things start to change. First off, I look around and find it really strange that a Try Vegan PDX bar crawl's first destination is held at a bar where dead animals hang on the wall. This only further drives home one of my theories about Portlanders sometimes being disingenuous. Though many of the people here do things they claim to stand for, some just don't seem to take a vegan lifestyle very seriously, as evidenced by this first vegan pub crawl bar with dead moose on the wall.

As I am sitting at our table, still having a good time with the South Floridian's phone in my hand, it happens. On his iPhone, a man I don't know sends a text that pops up saying, "Dude, you are such a dog!" I start to feel uneasy.

This random text catches me off guard so I click it open. Turns out this son of a worthless Ft. Lauderdale bitch I am with had snapped a picture of me naked during my 10-minute nap, and forwarded it to one of his buddies.

You can see my entire body, fast asleep, in this shot. I call him out, and he's speechless. He can't come up with an excuse to save his life. I get upset and start to walk outside. He follows me but has zero explanation for his inexplicable behavior. I want to know why he would do this, especially since he kept claiming he wanted to hang out with me for the rest of the week.

The photo was wicked hot, don't get me wrong, but he had no permission to take it, let alone send it to a buddy for fun. The worst part was his caption with the picture, saying, "She can't keep up." I take one 10-minute nap during my two days with him and feel betrayed.

I want to scream as I leave the bar, but don't. He follows me onto the street. I call him out on what a sleazy ass he is for doing such a violating

109

thing to me. I feel let down by my friends who introduced me to him and finish the fucking pub crawl, ignoring him the rest of the night. I expected more from this Floridian who'd been a longtime vegan, someone I was encouraged to trust by our mutual friends.

He texts after I get a ride home and tells me he fucked up, and that I should find it in my heart to forgive him. He says he still wants to see me this week and hang out, and tries to convince me that we should. I resent him all the more for twisting things around, trying to make me out to be the one preventing us from having more good times.

I soon try to get in touch with the friends who introduced us and with whom we stayed, and they show a surprisingly underwhelming feeling of compassion toward me. They pretty much, for whatever reason, blame me because I didn't forgive him. I'm put off and disappointed by them, too. If I'd ever introduced one of them to an old friend of mine, had the roles been reversed, I would have been embarrassed and appalled if an old friend had pulled that kind of behavior on a newer one. I would have felt awful and sorry, but these people didn't seem to care.

Those friends and I don't really ever talk again. I try several times to just say I miss them, and try to work things out, but they don't respond genuinely. They make it clear they judge *me* from this episode, not him. It feels like a gender double-standard, where the woman is blamed for being a victim, and it's worse because they were good friends of mine. But I realize I can never really be friends with them moving forward.

I feel disappointed by these "friends" and toward yet another man I met in Portland. I think I have nothing left to text back to this two-faced jerk, but after he again writes and says, "You should find it in your heart to forgive me," I reply to him that he should find it in his heart to actually have one. That's it. The interaction is over, and I am done with him quickly. And less than a week later, reflecting back on those couple days, I realize I actually *did* accomplish my goal, for better or for worse: to get drunk at the prom, and fucked.

CHAPTER 11

THE MANHANDLING DENTIST

"You have really nice teeth."
—The Manhandling Dentist

One of the best-looking men I've ever seen is eye-fucking me from the bar at the Doug Fir. I am about to see The Heavy with some friends in the club downstairs, though I can't help but look back at him. The Doug Fir is one of the coolest places to see music in Portland because the room is literally carved out of a tree. I've seen performers here from the amazing Alejandro Escovedo to wildly talented pianist Marco Benevento. There are fire pits outside in the cold and halls made of mirrors inside, and after a few you'll definitely run into yourself trying to find a bathroom.

This eye-fucking man finally comes over to our table and offers to buy me a drink, and I happily accept. He's impressed with my love of Jameson. He's in town for a wedding, and I say that I'm about to head down to see the show, and we exchange numbers. One of my friends tells me he looks like a soap opera star, another tells me he is the epitome of a sexy Alaskan woodsmen, and one of the guys tells me that men who look like that can pretty much get whatever they want. I just might be willing to give him whatever he wants.

The Heavy put on a wild, high-energy show, and I'm feeling quite energized myself, especially since this beautiful man has my number. He explains that he's a dentist, living in Southern Oregon. He spent many years in Portland but wanted to be closer to his family so he moved back, and that's where his practice is. He still has friends and family in Portland and often visits on weekends. He isn't wearing a wedding ring and says he doesn't have a girlfriend when I ask. After I get home, all I can think about is seeing him again, and fucking him. He texts me several times that night and into the morning.

He calls me early the next day, sounding as hungover as I feel. He asks if he can come over and I say yes, knowing Nomads will be at work. He shows up quickly, and he's even hotter in the daylight than I remembered. He has thick, dark black hair, long enough to pull onto, bright white teeth, and gorgeous green eyes. He's Irish, about six feet tall, and from looking at him, even with clothes on, I can tell he has a chiseled body. I tell him I'm about to make drinks, and he smiles.

He says all he wants is to drink and chill with me all day. Sounds like a pretty good starting-off point to me. We tell each other about our nights as we sip on our greyhounds and then we begin kissing and getting naked. He tells me how much he loves my eyes, and he wants to go to my room. I have my period, and instead of just saying no to one of the hottest men I have ever known in Portland, decide to see what he wants to do.

He tells me that since we don't know each other very well, he thinks we should wait until next time. He explains something about the amount of fluids that would be exchanged, and I realize he must see a lot of fluids as a dentist and use words like "fluid" often. We have a couple more drinks, talk and kiss, and soon it gets dark and he has to drive five long hours back to Southern Oregon.

The next weekend, he comes back to Portland for another wedding. Late summer here is so beautiful. We chat a few times, mostly on the phone in brief interactions since he isn't much of a texter, and on Sunday morning I get a very early phone call. He's lying in bed naked, hungover, and wants me to join him at his suite in the Hotel Monaco downtown. I've visited the Hotel Monaco for happy hour in the Red Star bar. I know the place well.

He uses the word "manhandle" when describing what he wants to do to me, and I have to call the Special Friend to ask him what exactly he means by this term. Certainly doesn't sound like dentist talk. The Special Friend tells me I'm in for another version of the Mister. Somehow, I manage to attract these men.

I put on a dress, cab it to the Hotel Monaco, and find him in the exact state he described. Liquor and beer bottles strewn about, clothes everywhere. It's a mess and smells of a man after a wedding, but the whole scene is a turn-on for me.

He leaves the door open so I walk right in. He wakes as he sees me and tells me how gorgeous I look. He asks me to take off my dress immediately and to get on top of him in bed. I do. He is even sexier than I remember, with strong arms and a perfect body. Another one of the strange words he uses is "calisthenics" instead of "work out," but clearly it's working for him. He grabs me hard and tells me to find the "intimacy kit" the hotel provides with lube and condoms. The thing I remember most is him fucking me hard from behind, with one hand around my neck and one gently pulling my hair, telling me to turn around and look at him, and I can barely breathe. I am in for some of the best sex of my life.

I think about the chapter in Ian McEwan's *The Comfort of Strangers* where you find out one of the women is in constant pain, not because her husband beat her like you think, but because he broke her back fucking her so hard one night, and it wasn't his choice to keep going, it was hers. So here we are, at Hotel Monaco in downtown Portland; not exactly Mr. McEwan's setting back in the day in an unnamed European place... but I think I can relate.

Later in the day he offers to drive me home in what he calls his "weekend car." One of his dental books is on the backseat. I'm relieved to see no car seats or toys. I did ask him about having someone in his life, and he said no when I first met him. Plus, there is no ring. I am hoping he'd be truthful if his "family" consists of a wife and kids in Southern Oregon.

After that day it's as if he disappears for weeks on end, and his random texts are few and far between. He is wishy-washy with plans we try to make for meeting up on the weekends he says he'll be in Portland.

But he and I do see each other several times during late 2012. One time after sex he's exhausted even though I want more, and he tells me how sexy I am. Then he blurts out, "You have really nice teeth." I laugh and say, "I've never had a cavity," and he laughs back, "That's impressive." He has perfect teeth himself, of course, along with everything else including his dick, which is pressed against me.

I figure since we are all cozy and worn out for a few minutes, I can ask him something I'd been wanting to for a long time. I sense him to be a bit of a flake and can't shake this feeling that he has someone back home. As we lay in bed, I ask if he's married. He is shocked and seems caught off guard and somewhat insulted. I should have prefaced it with something else. He replies, "Not even close."

And then I ask if he has a girlfriend, and he assures me, as he always has, that he does not.

He tells me he has been out of touch because he'd been moonlighting in Alaska (apparently dentists get paid more there), then in Guatemala (doing mission work), and he later decided to vacation in Costa Rica. Genuinely interested, I ask if he fucked some hot Costa Rican women; he looks confused and surprised, and again says, "Not even close."

He then asks if I have a boyfriend, and I tell him honestly I would never be sleeping with him if I did. He seems relieved. I tell him I'm not even interested in having one at this point. I explain that I want to be on my own, have my walks to and from work, enjoy my friends here, go on adventures, not have to answer to anyone, and not be let down by anyone anymore. I tell him I am using this time to write, and he is genuinely interested. He asks about what, and I tell him it's a compilation of vignettes, real-life stories about Portland. He says he wants to read it and then asks if he'll be in a chapter. I say, "Not yet."

He makes me laugh, we cuddle, and we talk about how close we both are to our families. I tell him how my grandparents met at the Covent Garden Opera House in London during World War II, and he tells me about his family being from Ireland. We talk about our heritages, and he starts calling me his "little Russian Jew," which I take as a compliment. I respect a man who is so close to his family and his roots.

He then asks why I was compelled to ask if he has a wife. I tell him I always ask men if they have a girlfriend, and it hasn't always worked in my favor. I explain the time I was trying to get over my soulless-fuck of an ex in Portland and met a gorgeous man at Slow Bar in Southeast. We ended up bar-hopping with some friends and having a sleepover. We never fucked, but we got naked and played, and even after I asked him more than once that night if he had a girlfriend, he assured me he did not, though he still left incredibly early the next morning. A few days later, I get a call from his wife. It turns out I had been asking the wrong question that night, and I learned my lesson. The Manhandling Dentist was interested, shocked, and sorry to hear that had happened to me.

Also at this point, I'd come to the conclusion that my soulless-fuck of an ex had cheated on me with *his* nasty ex who'd cheated on him. And that most everyone in Portland was cheating, especially the men, so I could never be too sure.

He seems to sincerely understand and kisses me. He leaves to go to a late brunch with some of his local family, and we talk later. He makes sure to call me on his long ride home and promises to come back to visit. We dirty text and talk on the phone from time to time. But deep down I feel I cannot totally trust him, after all I've been through. And I don't really have the energy or patience to find out.

It's around now I realize I'm not optimistic about anyone anymore. I start to feel Chad

Kultgen's *The Average American Male* isn't just about low-lifes but pretty much every male I have met here. In relationships moving forward, I will have a barrier around me because of the lack of honesty I've experienced again and again. Having been let down after being so trusting and investing my time in the people of this city, I am not quite the upbeat, positive person who arrived here little more than a year ago.

One weekend he is supposed to be here for a dental class and then see me, but I get some excuse from him about being sick, and my interest is quickly waning. He seems to always have excuses when he says he'll be here and then doesn't show up. He's just too unreliable. I will never be sure if he has someone back in Southern Oregon, but I still take him at his word.

He continues to text from time to time, telling me of his next arrival, and I tell him I'm not holding my breath. He tells me to "behave" whenever I give him an explanation of why I don't expect him to show up. I've decided it's not worth the energy to do anything but let these men have it on their terms. My lovely and wise housemate Nomads says it perfectly: "Whatever they're thinking is bullshit. They are almost like machines built for good sex, but that's it!"

I am starting to think she nailed it. I tried my best, and considering the track record these men have in this city, I wouldn't be at all surprised if he is lying about everything. I still give him the benefit of the doubt, though after a while I stop answering his calls and texts.

Autumn is ending, the rain is returning, and I lose any remaining desire I have for him. Around this time I start having bizarre nightmares that I am losing my teeth. This dream is commonly linked to anxiety, a feeling of loss, a lack of comfort. All these interpretations could apply to me at this point in my Portland journey, when so many people are letting me down and I am far from home. I just hope to never again hear the word "manhandle" from a hot dentist who tells me I have really nice teeth.

CHAPTER 12

THE OLD FRIEND

"There will always be you and me. What we have is something very special."
—The Old Friend

While visiting me in Portland, after many years of dating, fighting, laughing, heartbreak, hardship, and love, the Old Friend reveals that he fell for me in second grade when I was teaching him to play checkers. I beat him of course, while looking up at him with my big blue eyes and smiling, probably giving him the same look I do whenever I get to see him these days. Except now it's after hugging, kissing, and when he's holding me naked, while I'm cuddled up to his chest after intense sex. We understand each other more than two twentysomethings from the same small town ever should. And then sometimes we don't get each other at all.

We were always close growing up, and grew even closer in high school. At that time I was dating the captain of the football team, a prom-king type from a neighboring town. He's now a Republican living in Texas and married with a baby. Clearly we never would've worked out, and I mean that in the friendliest way possible.

But it's really when I take a semester off from college in 2006 (too many South Beach weekends, early morning honors classes, a demanding PR job, not eating enough, drinking more than enough) that the Old Friend and I begin seeing each other differently. We date that semester—he's at Bryant College and having a tough year as well. I'm taking online courses at Lynn University, classes for fun at UMass Amherst, and modeling, and we fall hard for one another. It's as if we need each other during these hard times, and we save each other from ourselves. Being together makes it seem like what we're going through isn't so bad; we keep each other pointed in the right direction, and happily. It's probably not the healthiest start to a relationship, but after so many years of friendship, it makes a lot of sense at the time.

For a year, we are in love. We go to my oldest cousin's wedding together, his sister has a baby, he graduates, and we spend a lot of time at my parents' house with their friends from New Orleans who are displaced after Hurricane Katrina. Lots of things happen. He lives on Martha's Vineyard that summer after graduation, and I visit him regularly. There are many nights spent on his back porch in Edgartown. I turn 22 at midnight in his bed there, having amazing sex (to the sounds of *Under the Table and Dreaming,* the only time I've ever tolerated Dave Matthews), the rain pouring down outside his window. After work, he'd bring home organic produce and tofu for me to cook up for dinner. It was lovely.

Come fall, I return to Lynn as a senior. With me back in Boca Raton, soon to graduate, he comes to visit. There are more beaches, nice dinners, and good sex... just a bit further south. I remember the day we laid out on beautiful Delray Beach soaking up sun, kissing, cuddling, taking pictures. We end up in a Spanish restaurant downtown. I get the vegan paella and he orders the meat version. The server comes back and jokingly says, "You two could not be any more different," referring to our meals. But she was onto something.

During this time, which I think is one of the best weeks we've ever had together, he's in another place and doesn't quite share my enthusiasm: we are too different at this point, he doesn't want to travel, be adventurous, or in a relationship... exactly the things I do want. A couple weeks after he leaves Boca, he calls and breaks up with me over the phone, like any genuine tool would do from 1,500 miles away, with 20 years of friendship and one year of dating behind us. And with no explanation.

I remember standing out on my balcony of the hotel I lived in at the time (one of the perks for Lynn University honors students), overlooking the pool that we had fucked in less than a month earlier, not understanding his decision at all. I remember Natasha, my beautiful roommate from South Wales, coming home to see me out there chain smoking cigarettes, crying to my parents over the phone, and blasting Kim Richey songs. She hugs me, says she loves me, and having just met the Old Friend, is as confused as I am. My heart was seriously broken, for the first of a couple times it will be by him, and it felt almost beyond repair. He and I don't talk for a long time, and I remember thinking during my graduation how he should have been there for me as I graduated valedictorian.

About a year later, I'm at a party back home in Massachusetts, and he's there. I don't remember later bringing some of the people back to my parents' home that night when they were away, but apparently I did. And I must have invited the Old Friend as well, wanting to talk or something.

I wake up in the morning, no clothes on, walk over to the living room futon that already has two near-naked friends of mine cozily snuggled up, and crawl in between them, asking who the hell was that in my bed. They tell me it's the Old Friend. I cannot fathom the thought of even talking to him, let alone sleeping with him that night. But, um, just like that, I had.

We have a very complicated and confusing friendship after that. He admits that since the day he broke up with me, he thinks about me every morning when he wakes up, and every night before he falls asleep. We fuck a lot, he lets me down a lot, I should have stopped it, but I didn't. I am living in Amherst, house- and dog-sitting for a family friend who's on a getaway in Australia that summer, as I recover from my car accident. He goes out a lot with other people, never inviting me to shows or parties, and seems only to want to be with me when he wants sex. Looking back during that time, emotionally, he did me more harm than good.

A friendship timeout is called, and then at some point we start getting along again. He starts treating me better. I am in the process of moving to Northampton and about to open my shop, Layla Vera. Before I know it, we start to date. I forgive him, somehow, and try to put the past behind me. We are happy together, again, and it just feels right. He helps me build my store with Ikea glass display shelves and furniture, listening to the first Vampire Weekend album in the background. We celebrate the holidays, go to concerts. I beat his friends at beer pong at their house parties, and very easily we are back in love.

He goes all out for me on New Year's Eve, taking me to my favorite Italian restaurant in Northampton, Viva Fresh Pasta, then to see Enter the Haggis at the Iron Horse Music Hall, and we ring in the new year with my crazy friends at the Northampton Brewery. I know he's not as fond of partying on New Year's Eve as I am, but he keeps telling me all he wants is to see me happy on a night I always love to celebrate. I remember him comparing these days when he leaves my apartment to the scene in *500 Days of Summer,* when Joseph Gordon-Levitt is leaving Zooey Deschanel's place after they have sex. There is singing and chirping bluebirds. It's colorful and cartoon-like, and one of the nicest things he could possibly say.

Around the one-year mark, just like clockwork, he has family issues he needs to tend to. I want to be there for him in every way. Selflessly and honestly, I try to do that more than anything, but he doesn't appreciate or really even respect my efforts. He won't even talk to me for weeks. It's as if we are not together anymore, and I am holding on so hard to be there for him and his family. He doesn't want it. His mom sees and talks to me more than he does.

The Old Friend has no hesitation when I tell him we shouldn't do this anymore, and just like that comes another period of separation. We break up (again) after I wake up one morning next to a man I met at Tunnel Bar who comforted me the night before. I had no choice but consider our relationship already over as the Old Friend hadn't really communicated with me in nearly a month. Sadly, I could finally accept it.

But when we are eventually ready, the Old Friend and I become friends... again. We cannot *not* be. It would take something more powerful than us to keep us away from each other permanently, regardless of space or time or the past.

When I am about to move to Portland, I know I want him in my life, and he wants me too. I spend my last night in Massachusetts with him; we know each other so well that the sex is ridiculous, and we get each other completely. There is an understanding at this point. After all the fuck-ups, apologies, hurt feelings, happiness, connections, and the sex, I know we still mean more to each other than any of that. And he is trying to be a better man… I can see it.

He is the one who checks in on me day after day when he hears about my bad break-up in Portland. The Soulless Fuck I was serious with for months managed to make me more jaded than the Old Friend ever has, and the Old Friend understands this. I think he felt a responsibility to check in on me, helping me through, because it was not so long ago that he did the same thing to me, breaking my heart. He genuinely wants me to be happy again. At times, he's one of the few people who can make me feel true happiness.

The Old Friend is one of the guys who show up on Pad's doorstep in Portland, about a year after I get to Oregon. He arrives with a mutual friend, from kindergarten, who was my neighbor growing up. I remember when my neighbor used to sing "Last Night" by the Strokes at lunch every day of high school senior year, standing on a shaky cafeteria table, air guitar and all. The neighborly rock star and I even had sexual relations. In my parents' home, on their deck in the rain, after a summer of college. We'd be chain smoking, chain drinking, chain music exchanging for a whole day or more; he made me listen to Tokyo Police Club over and over again, and one thing leads to another.

But seeing the Old Friend in Portland is in a league of its own. We are 28 now, we are lovers, we are friends, we can communicate through eye contact, and the bottom line is we miss each other. Buzzed one night in bed that week, he tells me he loves me. He also says that I am perfect. (Did I mention he was quite buzzed?) But it is not unlike the way he told me he loved me the first time, after we came home from a party at Bryant College and we were 21, in his bed. Before all the nonsense we've put each other through. He also says, that night in Portland, that the thought of being with me again is not out of the question. He thinks about it, and this makes me smile, for whatever reason.

In Portland, the Special Friend, my neighbor Brenna, and my co-worker Devan comment about the way he looks at me and how he touches me. The Special Friend says he sees the love, and Brenna says we are soul mates. I half-jokingly tell them to keep their comments to themselves. But I am sure the bartenders at Rogue Distillery and the Conquistador Lounge could see it as well. We all have a great week, the Neighborly Friend, the Old Friend, and me. We end it at Portland City Grill in style, and there the Old Friend starts to withdraw, acting quiet and distant. He's not particularly affectionate, even though he's been all over me the last few days. It's an all-too-familiar pattern, and it still stings.

After that happy hour at PCG, the Old Friend and the Neighborly Friend drive me to Portland International; I'm leaving on the redeye to go to my cousin's wedding at the Omni Parker House in Boston; the boys are headed up to Seattle. It'll be the first time I'll be visiting back home on my own

128

since moving to Portland. Any other week, I'd be counting down the minutes to when I'd be landing and seeing my family, friends, and Northampton; but this is a moment in Portland I don't want to leave. These boys I grew up with, here in my new city across the country, the whirlwind of good times we'd just had. And despite his behavior, I'm not ready to say goodbye to the Old Friend, knowing it will probably be another long while before seeing him again. At the airport, I tell him I love him, he smiles and says it back. We kiss, and it's almost too hard to turn away.

Not long after that, he moves from Amherst to Cincinnati, career goals to achieve, and barely communicating. He's always had a self-centered quality that makes us very different, and that's probably the source of our biggest disconnection. We take another break from being friends, as smart people should when they just aren't making each other happy. But when you want it so badly, it hurts.

Then there is a night in one of the cigar bars at the McMenamins Kennedy School (a very cool older school building that has turned into multiple restaurants, bars, music venues, and lodging) in Portland with two of my close girlfriends here, housemate Nomads and friend Dane. I'm talking about men, drinking Jameson, smoking a vanilla-tasting cigar, and one of them asks an out-of-the-blue question: "Jess, of all the men you've been with, who is the most beautiful one you have ever known?" For fuck's sake, if you're reading this, you know there have probably been quite a few I can choose from, but I don't hesitate. I answer immediately, my tongue can't help itself. I say the Old Friend, just like that. No contact for months, not anything to prompt me. But that was my honest answer at the time.

The next morning I wake up in my bed, reeking of cigars and whiskey, and have the Mister coming over for some Sunday Funday fun. But before I can think of any of that, I text the Old Friend, "Hello." He immediately replies, "Well, hello."

The power of hello. I explain to him the question I'd been asked a few hours earlier, and my answer. And he tells me that this puts a smile on his face. He says, "It's not everyday someone hears something like this."

He also says he thinks I was clearly mixing crazy juice with my Jameson last night. He knows me too well. I tell him how much that makes me laugh, naked in bed, and just like that I miss him. He says he does too. We have phone sex, catch up, quote entire *Seinfeld* episodes, and hardly skip a beat. We make each other laugh, make each other come, and our friendship, via Cincinnati and Portland, is back.

We will always have this inexplicable and indelible connection. It can't be broken, but it can be damaged. We have damaged it many times, and that is what makes every time we repair it even more remarkable, since it seems to make us closer. It's what makes this different from other friendships. When I ask him if we will see each other again soon, the answer is always, "Hopefully."

Over the phone when I tell my dad for the umpteenth time that the Old Friend and I are back on good terms, he is happy. He's always liked him. But for the first time, my dad interjects that if the Old Friend truly got me, everything I am, he would be with me, begging to be with me, and he's simply not. I get his point. I don't necessarily want marriage, or kids, and neither does the Old Friend. But I'd like to be myself with someone who will make me happy, appreciate me, and let me reciprocate. My dad says, "If the Old Friend doesn't get that, he doesn't really get you." Maybe the Old Friend is just not capable of giving his all to me, or to anyone for that matter.

I talk to him after that conversation with my dad. I say, "I love you, and I miss you." He says, "I miss you too." I say, "Tell me you love me." He says, "I love you like one of my closest and oldest friends." I say, "You can tell me it without everything else, I get it." And he says, "I love you." We have phone sex afterward, and he tells me I'm the most beautiful woman he knows, inside and out, and it always has been me. I love hearing this from him, and probably always will.

I guess that's why I so easily answered that question in the cigar bar. I don't know if the Old Friend and I will end up with each other down the line, or if he'll settle for someone else, or simply want to be alone. I will be over the whole thing in time. There are other men, other cities, and I'm pretty much at that point now. But I do believe that what we have is unconditional. I do not necessarily believe there is one person for everyone, and he is probably not the one for me, but I will always love him, like one of my closest and oldest friends.

CHAPTER 13

THE SPACE NEEDLE AND THE LESBIAN TRYST

"You are such trouble."
—The sexy engaged girl I hook up with in Seattle

The weekend before New Year's Eve 2012, my dear friend Colleen is visiting from Massachusetts, and a few of us decide to go to Seattle for an overnight. I have never been, and Colleen has friends there so it promises to be a good time.

Colleen and I met in 2009 when I owned my shop in Northampton, and she worked in the store next to mine. We'd throw paper airplanes over the ceiling-beam tops to one another and hit up the Northampton Brewery and Sierra Grille after work. The epic messes we made throughout

133

Northampton, and later in Boston where she now lives, won't soon be forgotten.

The thing I first love about Seattle is the drive into the city. I have a tendency to get emotional butterflies in certain places. I get them weekly here in Portland when seeing the Old Town sign over the highway, or seeing the CITGO sign in Kenmore Square in Boston, or seeing the signs to Boca Raton when leaving the Palm Beach International Airport. The most overwhelming of these feelings hits me as I approach the George Washington Bridge whenever I get to New York City. There is that moment when the city is larger than life itself. The energy and happiness is palpable. Tears well up in my eyes every time.

Seattle is small, but I still feel a thrill driving into its rainy gloominess. It is very Portland-esque in a big-sister way.

We start our busy day barhopping around downtown before meeting up with Colleen's friends at their beautiful, grown-up apartment that has a gorgeous view of the city and directly faces the impressively large and phallic Space Needle from the balcony. The couple that live here are fun, generous, and engaged, and everyone hits it off immediately. With some Crown Royal and beer, the night begins to unfold. It feels like I'm in a *Frasier* episode.

Six of us have dinner at Terra Plata, a beautiful restaurant in Capitol Hill, and we later end up in a random bar's private karaoke room with a bunch of inebriated Asians, together singing our lives away. At one point I think they playfully try to kidnap me, and eventually I leave the bar without my purse.

I end up safe and sleepy in a guest bedroom in the grown-up apartment of the couple we went out with, and before I know it find myself hooking up with my new friend, the girl who lives there, her fiancé asleep in the next room.

She's putting me to bed, and my Jameson-filled brain can think of nothing else but having her. I'd had a similar thought earlier in the evening, and now in this bedroom with her, I want to make a move. The next thing I know I am pulling her toward me, and we are making out. It is soft, hot, and awesome.

I wake up the next morning alone, wearing pants that are not mine and nothing else. Opening my eyes, I look out the window and see the beautiful city of Seattle, sun shining and all. What a perfect first time in this delicious city!

I had never really been seriously interested in women until this past year. Could it be I've just run out of men? But I have a crush on the bartender at P.F. Chang's in the Pearl, where my Special Friend and I go every Monday. She is beautiful, with dark hair and sparkling green eyes. She hooks me up with free hot sake and makes intense, piercing eye contact with me whenever we go in. The Special Friend gets a little jealous every time. Our flirtation has turned to hugs, telling sensual stories about massages, sharing a love for Olivia Wilde, and her inviting me out to parties. We are getting somewhere.

Um, except she has a boyfriend. I fantasize about the day I can maybe have a threesome with her and her man (though I have not yet met him). I've never done one because I've been told by men that I'm too much to handle in bed on my own, and I don't think I'd be the sharing type while fucking. In all honesty, I think sex is super special and should just be between one lover and another. But I might do it just to get with her.

The only other time I really wanted to go to bed with a girl was at my cousin's wedding at the Omni Parker House in Boston. The wedding band singer, Haley, is a Brandi Carlile look-alike, and I badly wanted to take her back to my room that night. While she was packing up equipment, I ended up at the Beantown Pub next door with lots of wedding guests. I'd invited her to join us, I think, but didn't see her again.

The wedding was a little hectic for me because I had taken the red-eye from PDX to Bradley, drove straight to Boston with my family in the morning, spent the whole day strolling around the city, and then arrived at the affair with zero sleep and lots of miles under my heels. All this after not going to bed for the three nights prior, back on West Coast time, because the Old Friend and my Neighborly Friend, guys I'd known since kindergarten, showed up on Pad's doorstep earlier in the week. And I do have a day job.

My brother's girlfriend, Madz, asks me at the wedding brunch the next day if Haley and I hooked up or if I just dreamed of her all night. Sadly, I have to tell her the latter is true. As beautiful as it was, that wedding, on so many levels, made me feel incredibly lonely.

The morning after the wedding, I meet up with Colleen (now living in Boston) at the Beantown Pub, and we drink our weight in screwdrivers and Bloody Marys while catching up. This is the first time I've seen her since moving to Portland a year earlier. We chat about everything from love, work, special friends, and sexcapades to my newfound attraction for women. At this point, the gorgeous best man from the wedding stumbles in and sits next to me at the bar. I cannot believe how I didn't try to get with *him* after all our wedding dancing, and realize maybe this surprising appreciation I'm having for women is getting serious.

So when I wake up that sunny morning in Seattle, giddy and a little nervous, I'm proud that another chance with a woman didn't totally escape me. I shower alone, and then my new girlfriend and I do our makeup together and get ready for brunch. I think I could truly be happy in life with a woman at this point, with someone who isn't engaged to be married to a man.

We have an hour wait at a brunch hot spot called Skillet, but no one seems to mind as it's bright and warm outside. We rarely get this balmy weather the last week of December in the Pacific Northwest. Hell, we rarely get this weather at all, so we soak it up.

I call my dad and tell him all about my night, but not what happened with my new friend. I had him say hi to her, and they chat away for a good

15 minutes, everyone thinking she's actually talking with her own dad. Then she hands me the phone and I go to a nearby alley, telling him I hooked up with her the night before. He said she sounds very smart, really comfortable to talk to, and is happy for me. He thinks the whole thing is quite sweet.

Throughout the day, our little Seattle group of six from the night before barhops, and before heading home we end up at a high-end Tex-Mex restaurant. I really want to talk to my new friend about what happened. This place has huge "coke-friendly" bathrooms (thank you South Beach for my radar). They are private, with floor-to-ceiling doors made of wood. I follow behind her when she goes in one time, and as she's coming out, I nudge her back in.

I make small talk and then try to bring up what happened. She says it was fun and that I definitely initiated it, and my buzzed and happy brain wants her again so badly I can't help myself. I gently back her against the wooden bathroom wall and start kissing her. Her lips are so soft, and she tastes sweet like the alcohol we've been drinking. She keeps whispering, "You're so bad, you are such trouble," while smiling and kissing me back. I know her fiancé is at our table, and that he probably knows what is happening, and we stop. But I want more.

With barely a day to spare before 2013, I actually had my first official lesbian experience. Friends of mine all lost bets on this one, guessing dates well into the new year. I now consider myself an equal opportunist when it comes to sex, and I would happily be with a woman again. If my favorite bartender ever gives me the okay, I would get on her in lightning speed. Coincidentally, the girl from Seattle and my P.F. Chang's bartender could pass for sisters. I always have a type, male or female: tall, long dark hair, and piercing eyes.

From Seattle we drive back to Portland on December 30, really late. I'm at my office far too early the next day, daydreaming about the trip, about the girl, and wishing I could have stayed for New Year's Eve. The thing I start realizing from this experience, beside how awesome it is to fuck around with a girl, is that I do much prefer a man to make me fully satisfied. There is something about their hardness, fullness, and heaviness that I enjoy. A man's aggression, touch, and noises, are what I truly crave. But I tell myself I'd be happy with a man or a woman in Portland tonight for my midnight kiss, and perhaps even more.

Gazing at my work computer, I recall the previous morning, waking up in that gorgeous, grown-up guest bed: topless, slightly hungover, and smiling about my new experience. I can't get that moment out of my head. It's similar to a *Lost* flashback when a sign or image vividly etches itself in a memory. I can't stop thinking of the day before, when I was sleepily rolling over, opening my eyes, and gazing out the guest-bedroom window. There, directly in front of me, as if magnified and boasting, looms the phallic Space Needle itself... large and in charge.

CHAPTER 14

THE SPECIAL FRIEND

"If my situation were different, I'd fall in love with you in a heartbeat and it would be amazing. But given my reality, I'm content with our friendship."
—The Special Friend

I didn't start having sex with my best friend in Portland until my 13th month here. When I met him shortly after I arrived, he was disentangling from a woman, his ex. I'd met her on my infamous Portland vacation, and when I later moved here she quickly introduced me to her soon-to-be ex-husband.

At the time, she'd suddenly wanted a divorce and started sleeping around with everyone in the downtown Portland party scene. They had several children, and he seemed beyond confused and devastated as he thought about what this would mean for his future. He felt completely fucked over after devoting his life to this woman and their children. But he continued to let her treat him poorly and take advantage of him. I could never understand how weak he could be with this woman who had hurt him so badly. It is an unattractive quality to see someone get walked all over. Especially someone I am beginning to care so much about.

His ex and I don't remain friends due to her deplorable antics, but the Special Friend and I easily clicked after meeting. He and I soon find ourselves saying good morning to each other and texting constantly about the details of our days. He starts to pick me up every Monday, and we develop Monday Funday routines with trips to P.F. Chang's/Powell Books/Whole Foods in the Pearl District, and cozying up with *Lost* so we can re-watch the entire series from the beginning. Mondays were always cherished as he wouldn't have his kids, the one day we'd both look forward to after the weekend. I would fill him in on my latest escapades, and he'd be ecstatic to be out of the house with all the dizzying family drama going on.

Every other weekend (when he is kid-free) we party downtown at Kells Irish Pub or in Southeast at the Conquistador Lounge, crawling distance from Pad. We love dancing our faces off together and coming home to crash in my bed. Sometimes we prefer to just relax with beer, good food, and such movies as *Match Point* or *Closer* at my place. I introduce him to Dawes and Dylan, *Argo* and *Casablanca*, Chris Matthews and Bill Maher,

Chad Kultgen and Fitzgerald. We start grocery shopping and cooking together and become genuinely and affectionately attached. But not in a romantic kind of way.

With the recent past of his breakup, he couldn't even think about getting into another relationship. At least not for a while. So I don't think about us sleeping together in the beginning. Besides, I truly cared about him as a friend. The Special Friend's complicated past life with several kids and an unfinished divorce from someone very hard to reason with is a bit much for most people. I know if I didn't know him like I do and found out about his situation, it would be too much for me. But I believe he's a genuine good guy. His life got totally turned upside down... yet it's astonishing how he tries to be positive despite it all.

I start to let him sleep over a lot, and I know he really loves the calm and the company. We'd cuddle, but not too close at first. And the more we get to know each other, the more intimate the cuddling becomes, but always with clothes on. I liked to keep my distance so he wouldn't get any frisky ideas. Soon we spend every night together when he isn't with his kids. When we're not together, we talk and text constantly about anything and everything. He's become my best male friend here, truly a special friend. We start to really understand each other.

Two months after we meet, I take him to his first Wilco concert for his birthday, and we spend $70 on Jameson and six dollars on food next door at the Heathman Hotel before the show. While the solid opening act, White Denim, is performing, I convince him it is Wilco and he believes me.

When Wilco actually comes on to play, he is blown away. My plan had worked, so he could get the most possible out of the show. (It was like two headliners, I later joked!) I let him hold my hand that night. We kiss and sleep in my bed next to each other. I still tease him about Wilco, and he's always appreciative for that birthday together. He says he will always remember how I held his hand, and how I kissed him. I still remember the shivery and surprising feeling I got when it happened. It was like an electric current went through me, and I stopped it for all the reasons I knew I should.

On my own first birthday eve in Portland, he takes me out to one of my favorite spots, The Sweet Hereafter, and buys me my favorite oversize mason-jar drinks and heavenly vegan cake. We cuddle up that night, and I begin my birthday at midnight with someone I really like.

The Special Friend has seen me cry my eyes out over men, and he's seen me at my silliest, laughing beyond comprehension when I am high. I have held his hair more than once as he's thrown up in my toilet from too much booze, and he's met the Old Friend and the Neighborly Friend from my childhood. Not to mention the Mister, the Soulless Fuck, the Godfather, and many other men I've been with.

Soon into our friendship, he and I can be 100 percent ourselves around each other. There are no judgments, no insecurities; it's pure, honest, and loving when we are together. I've given him hell for making stupid decisions regarding his ex, and he's comforted me during more than one of my meltdowns.

He helped me move from the Kearney Curse to Pad in Portland, retrieved my stuff from the Soulless Fuck when we broke up, took care of me when I needed him after that breakup, and I would do anything for him in return. He admits that before I came into his life he wasn't having much fun, didn't have many friends, and was pretty miserable. I love to make him laugh and show him a good time. I tell him details about my romps with men and he listens, laughs, and attempts to give advice. He is quite shy, but he says that I bring out his extroverted side.

We go dancing, drinking, and dining out a lot. He meets my parents when they come visit me, and they adore him, of course. We play a lot of mediocre pool, explore bars like it's our job, but never once in that first year do we fuck when we sleep together in my bed.

But after a while feelings change, seasons pass, and gradually by the end of 2012 we start making out a lot. We spend some of New Year's Eve at what would later be known as "the Bogtender's bar" in the funky Stumbling Blocks neighborhood, and pictures are taken of us going at it in a booth with one of my breasts hanging out. Classy. He's my New Year's Eve kiss at midnight at a Pink Floyd tribute concert on Hawthorne after my Seattle trip. Clearly I didn't hook up with a girl that night after all. There's folklore predicting that the person you kiss on New Year's Eve will help set the tone for the coming year.

Very early on New Year's Day, Nomads and I drunkenly cook our guests authentic Sri Lankan cuisine—red lentils and red rice—back at Pad. The Special Friend announces he's Irish and loves rice, mistaking rice for potatoes. From then on every drunken late-night meal in Pad will fondly be known as "Irish Rice." The Special Friend and I crash in my bed, like we have innocently done many times during the past year.

I don't know if it was the Jameson, the moon that night, or both, but one March weekend before St. Patrick's Day 2013, we decide to consummate our friendship. I think I initiate it and didn't think he'd be as good as he is. I didn't think I'd want to keep going, but he came quickly and I wanted more. He promises to last longer next time, and we fall asleep.

We go out the next night and joke around about it. Nothing has changed in our friendship, and that's the most refreshing part about it. When I tell our friends, they ask if we're going to start dating, and I'm pretty sure I blurt out "Fuck no." He laughs and quietly agrees.

We start having sex regularly. He's more gentle than what I am used to, he's sweet and nervous and doesn't smack me around, unless I ask him to, and then I'm appreciative of it. I tell my mom we started sleeping together and she says, "Well, we all wondered when that would start." When I tell my dad, he says, "Whatever

145

works." I tell him how good The Special Friend is in bed, and he replies with, "You just never know." Words of wisdom.

Our relationship has become even more special, more respectful, and more fun, and I appreciate him more than I thought possible with any man here. He's been the one man in my Portland life who has not only been here for me, but has been trustworthy, someone I can call family. I wish his situation was different, but had that been the case, perhaps he wouldn't be who he is now, and we wouldn't have what we have. But I really can't stand his pre-existing conditions, that twisted relationship with his ex and their kids.

My female friends in Portland know him well through our relationship; one of his adorable and admirable qualities is his sensitivity, similar to mine, and my friends want to make sure he is able to disconnect sex from our friendship. They advise me to talk to him every time after we sleep together because they know he loves me, they know he is in love with me. I assure them he isn't, and that we have a mutual understanding. They respectfully disagree.

His physical attributes are not ones I'd necessarily find appealing, not at first anyway. But he is very cute, and his personality and the way he handles me are beautiful. I don't plan on staying in Portland forever, but whenever I leave, I know saying goodbye to him will be the hardest thing about going. We have developed a reliance on each other for support, love, and now sex. Some people argue that men and women cannot just be friends. But no matter what, I want to think we always will be.

One morning after a crazy tiki party with our P.F. Chang's bartender friend, the Special Friend and I awake together in my bed. I love morning sex, and afterward, I'm looking up at him. He smiles big, lovingly gazing at me, and says affectionately, "…those eyes," admiring my fresh-faced skin and big baby blues. I smile back. He sweetly kisses me on the cheek, says he has to leave to fix his car, go to his kids, start his day. I say goodbye, and I get it, and go back to sleep.

Three hours later, I wake up and realize he hasn't yet left. He is holding me in bed, all cuddled up close and peaceful. He wakes up sleepily and says how much he didn't want to move an inch away from me. I could tell he was relishing every second next to me. He makes me feel safe, and I realize some men really try deep down, and if *he* can get through what he is going through, no man or woman has any excuse for treating people badly. Beyond the crazy parties, drinking, fucking, good times, and hard times, the Special Friend has shown me that men can be decent, and they can even exist in Portland. Sometimes.

CHAPTER 15

THE MISTER, PART II

"You really do know how to pull off wearing a hat."
—The Mister (commenting on my green-velvet fedora in the midst of St. Patrick's Day craziness)

The day comes around when the Mister has a free afternoon. I'm watching *Seinfeld,* half-naked on my couch and the door opens so fast I don't even have time to get all the way down the stairs. He picks me up as soon as he gets to me, carrying me back up the steps as he undresses. He slams me down on top of him hard. He's still standing, my arms and legs wrapped around him, nothing to support us except each other. It's so sexy. We both come just like that in my living room, and he carries me to my room where we crash onto my bed. We laugh, smile at each other, and he asks, "So that just happened?!" We say how good it is to see each other. Then we talk a little bit about music, the East Coast, and fucking—the three topics we always seem to discuss passionately and without argument.

I see him a week or so later, at 10 o'clock St. Patrick's Day morning at his bar. The place is packed, and he is quite overwhelmed by the lines and the crowd. But as soon as he sees me in the throng, he hands me a Jameson, compliments my hat, and I yell back over the bar, "Thank you, I think I still have one of yours," referring to the straw fedora from the Oregon Country Fair I'd kept all these months. He responds over the loudness of the crowd, "I'm not worried, I'll get it back," and I shout back, "Maybe." He gives me this ridiculously sexy stare with those intense blue eyes, then smiles. I have to leave his bar immediately to take a breath with my friends in the fresh air of the giant party tent outside.

I don't end up with him that night, but I do talk to the Mister after St. Paddy's, and he tells me he really wants to work things out with his girlfriend. So I understand... again. It feels like we've been here before. He thanks me, tells me how amazing I am, and I don't contact him for a while. But the next time at his bar, things get a little messy.

My friends Sara and Megan and I go dancing at Barrel Room downtown, and then into his pub late night. He's kind of standoffish to me behind the bar, and I loudly let him know how fucked up that is, and then drunkenly end up making out with Megan in front of him. I apologize to him the next day, and he laughs. He says the whole thing was hilarious. Deep down, I feel confusion and resentment with all his flip-flopping.

When Grace Potter tickets go on sale for the Crystal Ballroom later that month, I buy one for Sara and one for myself. Then I text the Mister telling him tickets went on sale, remembering he loves Grace. He is appreciative of me being in touch with him. He proceeds to tell me how hard he got seeing my name pop up on his phone, how nobody fucks him like I do. I'm the best fuck he's ever had, he tells me again, saying he doesn't forget it for a second. It's great to hear from me, he continues, reminding me about the beginning of our last encounter, scooping me up, slamming me down on top of him on my staircase, and how he regularly jerks off thinking of that tryst.

I tell him I'm walking into a movie theater with the Special Friend and have to cut it short. It's *Silver Linings Playbook,* and I don't know why this movie has such an unrealistic ending, or why normal people going through tough times are made to look crazy. I think it's bullshit. People cheat, people die, and people react, and I know in my case, happy endings don't come around as easily or Pollyannaishly as they do in this film. I still consider myself an optimist.

I don't ask the Mister about his situation when we talk throughout the next few weeks because honestly it doesn't matter. Apparently he will want me regardless. He comes over immediately one afternoon, right after I tell him I'm seriously thinking of leaving Portland in the next few months. He thinks it's a good idea, and is happy for me. He feels I should be closer to my family, to Northampton, to the place I call home. He knows these last couple years for me in Portland were not so easy.

When we are on my stairs that day making out and getting naked, he gently asks me to not scratch his back. I think this might mean he's cheating on his girlfriend again, even though he told me this time they are definitely over. He tells me later it's because he walks around with his shirt off in front of his teenage kids when they visit, and apparently I leave marks, big ones. Strangely, every time I have the urge to really grab into his back, he sees it in my eyes, and lightly smacks me across the cheek. It makes for very good, rough sex.

This is where the term "the Mister" originally came from. The dominant/submissive relationship we had. I started calling him the Mister early on, and he relished that title. He always said how he got so turned on and excited when I called him that in texts, and how eager he got when I said it to his face.

After we both come a couple times that day, we are lying in my bed and he wants to talk. He pours out his heart about his now ex-girlfriend, and how he loves her still but found her cheating on him in bed with his co-worker one night. I look into his big blue eyes with my own, and tell him he's a piece of shit.

I ask if he forgot that he's been cheating on her with me this whole time via texting and showing up at Pad, and he looks dumbfounded, claiming he's never thought of it that way. I call him a piece of shit again. He says he really tried to make things work with her and just couldn't. I ask if he cheated on her with anyone beside me. He looks at me and tells me the exact dates he'd come over to fuck me while he was with her, and how he never seriously desired anyone beside me. And even if he had, he wouldn't have had the time. I have to believe he's not lying about that. I ask if she knows about what he did, and she doesn't.

He's the luckiest son of a bitch alive to get away with all he does. I tell him he never really loved her or else he wouldn't have cheated. He knows I'm right; he's had true love before. I tell him he's trying to convince himself he wants to be someone he's not, and maybe can't ever be. He says he wants to be good and settle down, and I sweetly look at him and say, "But you're not good deep down. You're not the guy you think you want to be. Seriously." He looks at me with piercing blue eyes and says, "Thank you. No one has ever told me that straight up, and you're right."

He knows everything I'm saying is true. He's trying to force something, fake it. But he loves fucking younger women, being a bar manager and a musician, and wants to think he loves the idea of love and companionship. But don't we all.

A few minutes later, the Mister confides that he had a vasectomy nearly a decade ago. I happily high-five him for this. The woman he was dating

152

was in her 30s, wanting to get married and have kids. I don't know what either of them was doing with the other, but clearly it wasn't meant to be. I tell him she always would have resented him for that, and apparently he didn't see that coming either. He kisses me and then genuinely says, "You'll meet someone back on the East Coast within a year, and you'll change about not wanting to get married and have kids." And even though he is not the first to tell me this, I insist that's not going to happen. I just want him to fuck me again, and he does.

Then he has to leave to go to work. He says he'd like to take a shower and wants me to join him. With the hot water pouring all around us, we joke about my lavender-smelling sheets and body gel. He tells me how smart I am, how grateful he is to me for giving him such honest advice, how he loves fucking me, how today was much needed for him, how awesome he thinks I am. Then we joke around about how he thinks he's getting old as he's about to turn 40. We laugh as I wash his back, gently, and he tells me how good it feels. I want to talk about anything beside his situation and turn to something we both love: music.

I tell him about the many upcoming concerts I have tickets to in Portland, including Dawes, The Mowgli's, Jim James, Family of the Year, Dr. Dog, Alex Clare, and of course Grace Potter. He says that missing these shows is killing him. I tell him he should just hang out with me more often, and he says, "I know, believe me, I know." He asks if I heard about the Waterfront Blues Fest

153

this summer featuring John Hiatt, Robert Plant, Robert Randolph, Mavis Staples, and Taj Mahal, to name a few, and I tell him I just got my tickets for the four-day affair.

He then reveals another secret. He tells me he only knows Grace Potter because when he was high one night at Bonnaroo years back, he saw her at 4 a.m. and she was hot as hell. I am so disappointed he doesn't even know her songs but tell him I wish Grace was in between us in the shower. He loves that. He keeps wanting to talk to me about his life, and all I want is to fuck him again, but I listen.

He gets out after our shower, and I stay in. He's already late for work, and after drying off he comes back in with me to confide one more secret. He says when he saw me at the Oregon Country Fair the year before, he wanted me badly. He describes my heels, the way I tasted kissing him, and how when I told him I lived in Portland, he actually wasn't going to call me because we'd probably already had our perfect moment together at the fair. He then confides how happy he is that he *did* contact me because a year later, look where we are. I don't say a word because I don't know where we are, or for that matter, what we ever were. I just look into his eyes and force a smile.

He gets out of the shower again, says, "Goodbye my dear, talk to you soon," and tells me how sexy I look washing my hair from the outside of the glass. And it's only when I hear my screen door close downstairs, moments later, that I begin to cry.

CHAPTER 16

THE ST. PADDY'S DAY DICK

"You can leave if you don't like it..."
—The St. Paddy's Day Dick

I see the Mister behind the bar of my favorite downtown Irish pub on St. Patrick's Day, and I'm ready for a morning shot of Jameson. My neighbor Brenna, housemate Nomads, and friend Sara are with me in the party tent set up outside for the holiday. We're acting silly in our green outfits, ordering drinks and swooning to the Irish dancers and music on the huge tent stage. Nomads and Sara have already completed the Shamrock Run for charity that morning, and they're amped for a good time. I'm looking forward to meeting someone and having my own marathon later on. Maybe it'll be the Mister, maybe not.

155

It's mid-afternoon when a beautiful 25ish man—tan, penetrating green eyes, and nice head of brunette hair—approaches our high-top table in the tent. I feel an immediate attraction, and we are quickly all over each other. He looks like he'd not been in Portland all year, with the brownish tint he has. We order drinks and talk about the band, which reminds me of the gritty pub-rockers I saw while studying in Dublin. He's quite flirtatious and makes my girlfriends and me laugh. His sister is with him, fitting right in, and we are all having a grand time.

Before I know it, I've been here for six hours. My head is swimming with Jameson and not enough food. A couple of my friends already left, so I want to go home soon. I invite this guy to come with me. His sister is suddenly very clingy, and she's giving him a hard time about leaving, which is kind of annoying. All of a sudden, she's overprotective and obnoxious.

He's ready to leave, though, and calls us a cab. We get to Pad, smooch, and fuck around. We talk a bit, I learn that his home is in Hawaii, and he tells me he's just coming off a break-up there. Nomads senses him to be sweet but a bit arrogant, and I have to agree. He seems like the type of guy who can basically get whatever he wants, and he knows it.

He wants me to go to another Paddy's Day party bar, but it's just about dark and I have to get up tomorrow at 6:30 to walk to work... and I *am* quite shammered. I don't even want to venture into the kitchen to make dinner. He says he'll call me. He texts me throughout the night, informing me of just what I'm missing, but I really don't care. I had a St. Patrick's Day in Ireland my junior year abroad in college, and nothing he says can convince me that one in Portland can compare to that. Memories of a messy Temple Bar scene in 2005, with Dublin pals Patrick and Rosie, are flooding my brain and I quickly fall asleep.

The next week he texts me after returning from a trip to Baja. He is coming to visit his sister again here in Portland. He says he wants to share some Baja stories with me and hit up some music that night. He also adds that he "wants to wrestle." I ask, "naked?" And he says yes. I find this kind of amusing. He invites me to join them at a club called Dante's Sinferno that Sunday night. I've always had fun there. It is a stripper/burlesque/magic/insanity/fantasy late-night world on Sundays, and I ask my friend Devan to join me. She and I meet up with him, his sister, and their posse of three friends.

Turns out I'm not the only one he's invited out that night who he's interested in. He blatantly flirts with some other woman he'd asked to come along, and she's clearly loving it. His sister is encouraging them to sit next to each other, and this woman is apparently a friend of hers too. This is starting to feel a little surreal. He insists to me that they are just friends, but Devan and I aren't buying it. And on top of his rude behavior, he is too-loudly cheering on the near-naked girls on stage, who are smoking cigarettes with their toes.

157

I start to get annoyed, and he ignores me. He's suddenly turning into the epitome of a pompous, privileged ass. I finally lose it as he's clapping and yelling crudely at the strippers, and a few seats away, he's all over the other girl he's invited. They are whispering, and he's acting like a drunk frat boy. He tells me I can leave if I don't like it. Taken aback, I simply tell him to "Go fuck off and die."

Devan and I leave, and I have a minor meltdown outside waiting for a cab. And I'd gone out at midnight on a Sunday to meet up with this guy. What a jerk.

I am disgusted by the men in this city. The ones I saw in the audience at that club are nasty and disrespectful to the performers, treating the dancers like objects. Isn't this supposed to be a talent type of show, not a sleazy strip club? I'd even taken my Mom here, and we always had a fun time. Is something changing in this city, or had I not wanted to see this much bad behavior before?

I never really got to know this guy from Hawaii, though he seemed nice enough at first. And he genuinely acted interested in me coming out to be with him that evening. Looking back, he never showed any truly endearing qualities, but I probably overlooked that when he was oozing charm under the St. Patrick's Day party tent.

Nomads later did some online detective research on this St. Paddy's Day dick and informed me the girl he recently split with in Hawaii was probably part of a native caste, members of which rarely date white men. Nomads wisely came to the conclusion that after he scored her—dating a native upper-class Hawaiian woman is a big deal for a white man—he felt entitled, thinking he deserved anyone and everyone he wanted. Despite that, she probably dumped him. Plus his sister obviously had an agenda for their friend, whom she clearly wanted her brother to be with that night at Dante's Sinferno.

It was another letdown. Somehow this slick dick and this city managed to put a damper on one of my favorite holidays... and that's not good *craic* at all.

CHAPTER 17

THE BOGTENDER

"The thing that sucks is that you and I together would actually raise really good kids."
—The Bogtender

My bubbly neighbor Brenna and I start frequenting a divey bar in the Southeast Stumbling Blocks neighborhood on Hawthorne every Friday. They make delicious vegan food—rice bowls with fresh veggies and curry sauces—and the drinks are stiff and cheap. The atmosphere is dark and cozy with wooden booths, pinball machines in the back, and one pool table off to the side. The food specials of the night are always written messily on a big chalkboard, and there is a ridiculous "Jell-O shot of the day" that we always get tossed. (I always hand mine to Brenna; Jell-O isn't vegan.) The crowd is eclectic, from men just off work to women who look like they have not changed party skirts in days. The bartender reminds me of a rough, tattooed, shaved-head version of the Mister. He has full facial hair, deep blue eyes, is about six feet tall, and looks strong. He reminds me of Woody Harrelson. I am oddly attracted to him.

We get to know each other, "the Bogtender" and me, and I start calling him this because there is something dirty yet sexy about him. Turns out he is the owner of this establishment where Brenna and I are now regulars, and this catches me off guard, not just because of his appearance, but because he is so humble. During the next few weeks, I meet his partners, his employees, chefs, and friends. He seems to have a thing for me, always flirting and hooking me up with free drinks.

I get to know him and his moods pretty well. He's almost always in a cheerful state, flashing a smile when we walk in and emerging from behind the bar to give us hugs. He's a teddy bear, sincerely sweet and sensitive beneath his rugged exterior.

One Friday, Brenna and I show up happily ready for the weekend, but he's not his charming, friendly self. I suspect something is off. He later tells us a buddy passed away, and everyone is here for a celebration/mourning of their friend. I should have realized this from the bar draped in black and girls sobbing in the booths.

A few days later, he asks me to meet him at his bar on his day off. It's early evening, and he pours us double vodka sodas with lemon. He tells me he's recently separated from his wife, and I am curious about what happened. It was mutual, he reveals, and I'm okay not knowing more than that for now. He's about 10 years older than me, and that night I talk about the shop I used to own in Northampton, and he explains how he acquired his thriving bar. We share an entrepreneurial spirit, among other things. We make each other laugh, and although he owns this bar, I'm never intimidated by the crazy yet amicable aura surrounding him.

I really like the scene here week after week. Everyone seems to know him, and he's always got loyal buddies at the bar with whom I talk regularly. A couple times we all go out to smoke weed, and everyone's cool and friendly. I feel right at home. Even the women always hanging around him don't alarm me.

That first time we are alone here on his night off, he looks directly at me as we talk, his sexy, sincere blue eyes contradicting that scruffy look. He touches me hesitantly on my leg and arm, and when I let him know it's okay, he is blatantly relieved. We hit it off and really start to open up with one another. We talk about our appreciation for President Obama, our parents, and certain parts of Portland that we love. We share our dreams of traveling and what we want for the future. When I tell him I don't want children, he tells me he's had a vasectomy.

I high-five him, but he looks at me sadly and sighs when I do that. And then, strangely, he says, "The thing that sucks is that you and I together would actually raise really good kids." This seemed a little forward at the time, and when I think of it afterward, it hits a nerve and stings.

We end up fucking that night in Pad, far too loudly. For the first time, Nomads tells me the next morning how out of control it sounded. It definitely started outside her bedroom before we even made it to mine. The sexual chemistry between us is electrifying. The Bogtender and I meet up again regularly over the next few weeks, at his bar and a couple more times in my apartment.

Hanging out a week later in Pad with Nomads, Devan, and Brenna, he brings up his ex and related baggage. It gets emotional talking about his past, we've had a bit to drink, but we fuck later that night, and very sweetly. I tell him I like him, and I try to think everything is okay. He leaves early the next morning. I go to work, but instinctually sense something is off-kilter.

I text him a couple times that week. I hope I didn't make things awkward telling him I had feelings for him, and I thanked him for always being so generous at his bar. I don't hear back.

He must have noticed two Fridays passing without seeing my friends and me. Shortly after, he texts me saying, "Hey, sorry I have been MIA. Me and my ex are trying to work things out. I hope there are no hard feelings." I tell him I didn't expect that, but there are no hard feelings. I also tell him, for what it's worth, that I had a lot of fun with him, and I wish him all the best. He says, "Yes, with you too, take care." This stuff doesn't really phase me anymore. It all feels so familiar, and I let it go.

A week later I have a dream about him. He must have been on my mind. I text him the next day, "Hey, I don't know if we are friends or not, but I had this really vivid dream that you were in last night. Anyway, hope you are doing well." I get no response and can accept that.

I think Brenna was the most disappointed as she doesn't get to go back to his bar with me again. I felt it would just be too awkward, and the main reason I went there is because the Bogtender was so kind to us, and fun. And for me, I am on the verge of my breaking point—not just with the men here, but with this city in general.

I start to realize how appreciative I am of the amazing girlfriends I have met here these past two years (Nomads, Dane, Devan, Sara, Megan, and Brenna). And then it dawns on me. They are all 26 to 36, beautiful, successful, intelligent, wicked fun, and unwillingly single, with strings of disappointing men behind them in this city.

Don't get me wrong, I met a couple women in Portland I wish I hadn't. But it strikes me strange that all the young women I've come to love cannot find decent guys to just date.

I have this overwhelming sense that there's a real lack of loyalty with these West Coast people, especially the men. Many I get to know come across as lost souls, and these aren't just transplants from California.

Maybe because a place like Portland is full of newcomers, flakiness is a mentality. But how does that explain all the men I met who grew up here? Do they develop it over time due to the influx of outsiders invading their city? They all seem to have parental issues to begin with because this is a place where kids having babies is the norm. This is perplexing and weird, especially because Planned Parenthood is widely accessible here. Is it me, or is this place a little colder and darker than I'd expected? Most men here simply display poor or lazy behavior toward women. Not to sound naive, but is that how it is in most places?

One evening at the Conquistador in Southeast Portland, near Pad, I propose a comparison of West Coast and East Coast people to a young couple I meet from upstate New York. They are having a bit of a problem meeting people as they've just recently moved here, and I tell them it took me a while to find as many genuine people as I did, explaining how many disappointments I had to weed through to find the gems.

My explanation went like this: If you meet people at a party in Portland, or some other West Coast city, they'll be cheerful, friendly, yet fake, but you'll take them seriously. You'll exchange numbers and they'll invite you somewhere tomorrow night. When you actually show up, they wonder why the hell you came. Did you really think they were being sincere? But in Boston or some other older East Coast city, you'll meet people at a party, exchange numbers, and they'll invite you out tomorrow. If you don't show up, they'll call you, wondering where the hell you are.

It may be a generalization, but I'm seeing a real pattern in this city, and I am starting to get cynical. I even start to think the weather back in

Western Massachusetts, as cold and brutal as it can be during the winter, actually makes people commiserate, and neighbors come together to help each other. It's a mentality, a sincerity, that started so long ago it's engrained in the East Coaster's DNA. On the other hand, the constant rain in the Pacific Northwest doesn't seem to do much other than make a lot of people dreary and distant toward one another. I can feel my heartstrings pulling me strongly elsewhere, and they're about to snap. I have to go back.

CHAPTER 18

THE SPECIAL FRIEND, PART II

"I've wanted this for a very long time. I haven't stopped thinking about you like this for two years now."
—The Special Friend

I didn't fall in love with my best friend in Portland until I lived here almost two years and had already decided to move back to Massachusetts. I don't know why it happened at such an inconvenient time, or why it hadn't happened sooner. Embarking on a relationship with him was never something I thought he wanted, and honestly it was never something I thought I wanted considering his overwhelming baggage from the not-too-distant past.

The time I spent in Portland has been very meaningful to me, but after two years, it is time to move on. I'm surprised I stayed as long as I did considering the turbulence, the first-world problems I experienced here, a few of which haven't even been mentioned in these chapters.

In the beginning, the situations I encounter are surprisingly challenging, and I wasn't fully prepared. I move three times in the first three months before settling into Pad with the lovely Nomads. Between the disgraceful people I live with early on and no immediate luck finding employment despite my work experience and business degrees, it was frustrating… but exciting nonetheless.

Finally, I found a good job, a wonderful apartment and roommate, and friends who become like family. But then I suffered a painful break-up with that soulless fuck I'd been dating for months. This after realizing he was, deep down, a lying, cheating loser. Part of me thought I'd return home then and there, but something was pulling at me to stick around. I wasn't ready to leave. I'm so grateful to my friends who made staying here better than I possibly could have predicted, especially as more obstacles continued presenting themselves.

Eventually I find myself desiring closeness to my family. My parents in Western Massachusetts, my extended family in Boston, and all the people I've known for years—they are beginning to feel too far away. I also miss the loyal qualities that seem more prevalent in the people I know back home on the East Coast. A friend from New York, who I'd met in Israel, said to me after I tell him I'm thinking of going back, "Isn't Portland kinda like the Northampton of the West?" And I reply, "It is, but not as special." I explain it doesn't have the neighborly closeness or collective progressive mindset. People are not as genuinely friendly. And 3,000 miles feels too far away from family. My friend appreciates this.

It is one weekend night in early spring after some tumult with that successful bar owner, the Bogtender, that the light comes on and I know my Portland stay is nearing an end. I probably should have just stopped trying to make it work in the love department but remained optimistic because he was kind and took good care of me. That is until he told me, via text, that he was getting back with his ex. I remember reading this and thinking how fucking old this kind of behavior is becoming. It's enough. I'm officially ready to move back to Massachusetts.

Early the next morning after that lame text, as I'm walking my two-plus miles to work, I hear on my iPhone earbuds the Green River Festival lineup being announced on 93.9–The River. This is the coolest radio station in Northampton and the surrounding Pioneer Valley, and it's where my brother works. I listen to it religiously on my walks.

Brandi Carlile is headlining one of the evenings at this family-friendly music festival that I've missed since being in Portland. Brandi is one of my favorite performers, and every time I've seen her it has been inspiring and uplifting. She'd even stopped by my shop in Northampton in 2009 before her show at the Calvin Theatre. I went to the concert with my dad, and it turned out to be the night before his mom passed away. "The Story" never sounded so poignant.

My dad texts almost instantaneously to tell me he heard the announcement, knowing what a big fan I am. I pull out my earbuds and call him back from the bustling Hawthorne Bridge: "I heard it too, buy me a ticket... I'm moving home then." He wasn't too surprised but sounded relieved. The festival is taking place during my birthday weekend in July, and I could think of no better present to myself. I arrive at work in a good mood, seeing an end to this Portland chapter in my life.

Shortly after this are the Boston Marathon bombings, and I feel more upset and disconnected from my family than I could have imagined. Close family and friends were there on Boylston Street that day, and just a year earlier, in the spot where the second bomb went off, my dad and our family had cheered on my dear cousin as she finished the race. Talking to loved ones back in Massachusetts made me feel I could not come home soon enough. I felt helpless and lost, just wanting to see their faces and hug them. It seemed no one in Portland, at least those I spoke with, could relate to the sadness I felt after that awful day in Boston. I went into work every day that week in a daze, unable to focus on anything except the latest news updates. Co-workers kept telling me to try and smile. Impossible.

I've always had a way of making big decisions. It probably started when I was very little and toddled over to the wastebasket in my parents' kitchen to toss away my trusty pacifier, never again asking for it. And it happened when I decided to move 1,500 miles to South Florida to attend school, not knowing anyone in that part of the country. As my parents dropped me off, I was so confident in my decision I barely said goodbye, or so they claim. It happened again when I sprung on them via phone that I was going to study abroad in Dublin my junior year, and again when I packed three suitcases to move cross-country to Portland after an adventurous hiking trek through Israel.

Dad visits me shortly after the Marathon bombings, and we are both thankful knowing this time we won't be saying goodbye for an indefinite period. We have a blast in Portland, going to WhiskeyFest Northwest and frequenting my favorite haunts Sweet Hereafter, Blue Monk, Jam on Hawthorne, and Portland City Grill with my friends. As much as I'll miss parts of this city and my new friends here, I'm ready to head east.

My dad isn't the only one not surprised by my decision to move back home. My friends in Portland, my bosses at work, even old friends in New York, D.C., and California get it. As do my friends and family in Massachusetts. They all sensed the inevitable.

When my dad is in town, the relationship between the Special Friend and me is starting to become real, and Dad encourages me to pursue things, to see what could happen with us. He says the way the Special Friend treats me and understands me is genuine.

This newfound feeling with the Special Friend is going to make things complicated in my ability to leave the West Coast, but I want nothing more than to give him a new life too, with love and happiness. He insists he has no family here, nothing worth staying for except his kids. He would never abandon them, of course, but I am bewildered by the decisions he and the soon-to-be ex-wife made, allowing them to get wrapped up in such a messy situation with so many children. He says he wants nothing more than to move east with me and will do everything in his power to make that happen. I tell him how frustrating it is, and he says, "No, it's infuriating."

He says he can't stand his life at times and is haunted by the poor choices he made a decade ago, ones that will affect him for at least another decade. He says he would move with me in a heartbeat if he could, and it's the first time in a long time I think realistically about a long-term relationship coming out of this Portland adventure. As improbable as that might sound.

It's not that I'd forgotten about his tangled and absurd situation; it's just that it no longer held me back from something I want. I get over the concern I have of losing my one true male friend here by having sex with him and being more than friends. He'd seen me at my worst and took care of me after other men in Portland let me down. He soothed me when I had an ear infection and got sick from the meds, and tended to me after I fell walking home from work and could barely move for a week. And he always told me I looked good.

Even when I was a mess, he said I was the most gorgeous girl in the room.

I know now the Special Friend wanted me from the first night we met on that wintry rainy 2011 night. A few of us had headed to a downtown club, and the Special Friend and I decided to leave after we'd heard one too many (meaning two) LMFAO songs. It was around the holidays. We ran into a Santa pub-crawl and were photographed with some crazed crawlers. I was in one of my holiday party dresses, and he said I looked like an ornament. He makes this sexual groaning noise every time we talk about that sparkly gold getup. He loved it on me.

That night, the two of us ended up at Henry's on 12th and talked until they closed. We were so cold walking around town that first night together, and I told him to softly chant "hot sex in a hot shower" because that always kept me warm. I think he was amused and looked at me in a way that suggested he was picturing us doing that. Although I'd meant it rather innocently, this blazing image was planted in our heads to help keep us from freezing in the rain.

That night I learned about the ongoing baggage with his ex and kids, and it made me see him as just a friend. We joke around now about that memorable night, and he says, "You had me at LMFAO."

Now, nearly two years later, I start telling Nomads I think I'm falling for him, and she tells me she already knows. She can tell. During this time I receive texts from Olympic, the South

173

Floridian from vegan prom, the Old Friend, the Manhandling Dentist, the Mister, and others. I'd started thinking less and less about those guys and more about the Special Friend. He saw this happening too, and it made him happy.

I remember one night at Powell's buying a few books, mine probably a Henry Miller and an Augusten Burroughs, his a Dostoyevsky to add to his growing classic-book collection that I eagerly encouraged him to start. I thought it was so sexy that he took my suggestion seriously. He started eating vegan at the restaurants we'd go to, and I started noticing how alluring his green eyes are.

He always opened doors for me, and then he seemed to get seriously lost while driving me around. One time he ended up in the beautiful Portland hills in Northwest, when we were supposed to be going downtown in a different direction. I made a joke wondering how we'd somehow found ourselves on Martha's Vineyard. He just smiled.

After a Mumford & Sons show at the Rose Garden that we'd walked to, I led us all the way back to Pad on foot. We joked later that had he attempted it, we'd have ended up on the Vineyard. He looked at me and said, "You know, I always got lost on purpose. I did it to spend more time with you." Although it was just his quirky sense of direction, the comment was kind and heartfelt. Little things like that crept up on me, and I couldn't deny that I was falling for him.

Lying on my couch one warm May night, I tell him I have a secret, and he says he thinks he knows what it is. He calls me out for being in love with him, and I don't say anything. He then says, "Well, you do know I am definitely in love with you." I start realizing this is what I'd craved all along on this crazy Portland roller coaster ride. When I start telling my friends and family about my newfound realization, they tell me it's about time because he's been wanting this for so long. I don't know why he couldn't have shared his feelings with me sooner.

I don't consider myself oblivious, but I know he didn't push hard enough to make me realize he was so interested, and that I should give us a chance. And his messy past had made it too much for me to consider having him as my own.

He starts saying such things as, "I love your beautiful big blue eyes, they kill me. I could look at your eyes and just see you smile and get incredibly turned on." He constantly compliments my beauty, sense of humor, kind heart, intelligence, loyalty to the people I love, and my attentiveness to him. He says I am the sweetest, most amazing woman he's ever met, and that no one has ever been there for him like I have been this whole time I lived in Portland.

Without our bond being friends, being 100 percent ourselves around each other, we'd never have developed the comfort and love we have. He even says although he lived near Portland his whole life, he never really saw or experienced it until I moved there from 3,000 miles away. He credits me with really showing him this city. Before I moved here, he was terribly unhappy in the suburb he grew up in, and going through hell because of his past decisions. The Special Friend says he never truly lived until he met me, and that I saved his life.

We could be out grocery shopping or dancing until 3 a.m.; in the sun during happy hour at White Owl Social Club; or just sitting on my couch for hours watching *How I Met Your Mother,* eating vegan ice cream, drinking vodka, laughing and having the best time. We are constantly telling each other to *"get out of my head"* as we finish each other's sentences. We have all the same jokes that we've developed during our friendship, like calling each other "8 Mile" whenever we wear hooded sweatshirts. And we cannot keep our hands off each other. The way he continuously smiles when he's around me, while grabbing me like he needs me more than anything, is the biggest turn-on at the beginning of an intimate relationship.

One day he confesses that the one short time he was seeing a girl these last couple years, he always wanted me. I tell him I don't believe it, and he says, "Jess, I took *you* with us on our first date, and almost every date I had with her after that. I always only wanted you." He explains how he settled for others because he truly thought he could never have me. Thinking back, I recall this one woman who kicked me under a table at Bunk Bar while the three of us were out. When I asked her if she "wanted to go pee with me," she thought I said, "want to compete with me?" He was clearly better off without that one.

I remember the first time he saw me naked before we started sleeping together. He had slept over after a crazy Jameson-infused night, and when I stood up, I had no clothes on. He was speechless. He managed to mutter "Damn!" without taking his eyes off me for a second as I walked to my door. Later he texts me saying how ridiculous my body is, how impressive, and how he thought it was fucking perfect. He starts making this *ooomph* noise when he finds me looking particularly sexy. When I remind him of that now, he says, "For the record, seeing you naked still blows me away every time. It still makes me sit back and say 'Wow,' and it always will."

After the first time we say we're in love with each other, the sex gets even better. The Special Friend calls it "earth shattering," "mind blowing," and "life altering." I totally agree. From hearing my stories the last couple years, he knows what I want. He kisses me better, holds me tighter, grabs me harder, and touches me sweeter than any man ever has. He also indulges in smacking me across the face a little harder than I ever have been, but he rubs my cheek before and after every time. He tells me he loves doing it because of the reactions on my face, the moans I make, the way I find the pleasure and the pain… and that turns him on. While he's pulling my hair and fucking me, he's always kissing me and looking into my eyes.

He knows exactly how to make me come by taking absolute control. It's perhaps the most control he's ever felt in his life, he can't get enough of it, and I relish in letting him. It feels

177

like we're making love and hardcore fucking all at the same time.

One evening in the shower, all steamy and dripping wet, he pushes me against the wall and shoves himself inside me. And then he just scoops me up on top of him. I wrap my legs around his body and he makes me bounce on him hard. It's hot and slippery, but he never makes me feel unsafe. I call it defying gravity. He has to stop himself many times from coming until finally I put my feet back on the wet floor and turn around. He then fucks me from behind, pulling my hair until I can't utter a sound, making me look at him, and he comes at the same time I do, deep inside me. We can't speak and collapse together afterward.

Later that day, I look into his eyes as he's touching me and innocently ask, "How did you get so good at fucking me?" He first corrects me, "You mean *making love* to you." And then he says, "I've been picturing doing it while I jerked off the last two years." I blush, turn away, not knowing what to say. But it was the perfect response. We joke now that he was taking notes the whole time. He tells me he's always wanted this kind of passionate sex, but was never comfortable enough with anyone to do anything that intense. He also says that no one he's been with would ever be into it. He told me after that shower that it was the first time he'd ever fucked in a shower. He says he never knew what sex was before me, and the way I give myself fully to him is unlike anything he's ever experienced.

Soon after that shower episode he shows up at my apartment after work one day. I have just finished laundering my bedding. I sprint down my stairs in see-through pink lingerie to greet him, and his jaw drops to the floor along with his work things. When we get upstairs, we attack each other. To keep the sheets clean for at least a little while, we start to fuck on my bedroom floor. Then he looks around my room for something. He grabs a small black satin belt out of my closet and pins my arms behind me while binding my wrists together with it. He says he "wants to do things to me that are illegal in most states," and I ache for it. That black satin belt will be used again...

The first weekend we are officially a couple, we go to Prost, a German bar on North Mississippi. It's a rainy Saturday, and we are sipping hot toddies and sharing Homegrown Smoker food (the best vegan food cart in Portland, and you can bring it into the pub!). He says he keeps having to stop himself from pointing out men at the bar he thinks are my type and would be good for me. It's endearing and cute and what he's always done for me. But I tell him, "I don't want any of them anymore." His sexy green eyes light up as he smiles, and he looks so happy. Then I tell him, "Because they're not you."

The next morning we head to Jam on Hawthorne for brunch, my usual routine with my neighbor Brenna, except she couldn't make it that day and he could. He confides he's always jealous of our weekend brunching and of so many things people his age do on weekends. Things he can't do because of his kids. We get screwdrivers and delicious tofu scrambles, and later relax on my couch watching *Entourage* for hours. He tells me this is the perfect day, and the first time he's ever really had brunch. This makes me laugh, thinking of the concept of someone never having brunch, and he looks me in the eyes and sadly says, "Well, it's the first time I have ever really *enjoyed* it." I promise to continue giving him new indulgences, from mind-blowing sex to brunch.

We get into bed later that Sunday afternoon, and I tell him he's the best thing that's ever happened to me. He reminds me he first said that to me a couple months after meeting me. Early in our friendship, he'd slept over on his birthday night after I took him to see Wilco at the Arlene Schnitzer Concert Hall. I held his hand that night, we kissed, but then I stopped it, and he was a gentleman. Now, all these months later when he says, "You are the best thing that's ever happened to me," I really hear it. And he continues to tell me that was the best birthday he'd ever had, and he will never forget how I held his hand and kissed him that day.

He credits me for encouraging him to start growing his hair longer, dressing nicely, eating well, learning about music, and caring about politics. He says he never knew what true love was before me, what real sex was before me, or what a loving family was. I want to give him all of these things because I believe he truly and finally deserves good in his life. I want to give him everything I can.

Within a few days of us being a couple, he moves into Pad with me. Nomads encourages him to stay here and bring his things over. She has always adored him. It is a possibility he will try to live here after I move. Before we became a couple, he was sleeping on his ex's couch (in a house he pays rent for, that her parents own) just to spend more time with his kids. Maybe he will still do that after I go.

He's always said he just wants me to be happy, that's all he's ever wanted. That's why he sat back during all the other men, because his friendship with me meant more than getting jealous. I can't understand how he possibly was so good at hiding his feelings, especially when I was with others. But after a few weeks of us being together, he shows twinges of emotion when we joke about the other men I've been with in Portland.

Friends who learn about our relationship via Facebook say, "finally" and "it's about time." The Mister genuinely congratulates me via text on my new status, and I let the Special Friend read our whole conversation, including the part where the Mister tells me I am "seriously the best fucking sex of all time."

I have no secrets, nothing to hide. I know with us being 100 percent honest with one another, things might just work. That's the only way there can be a future with us. And if not, we'll always have these two years... and these few months of *really* being together in this city.

Of course he tries to convince me to stay in Portland, but I just can't. More than ever, it's time to go back to my real home, and if he ever presented an obstacle to this, I might ultimately resent him. He says that's the last thing he wants. But he still can't wrap his brain around how amazing us being together is, and that I actually want him in this new way.

He plans to fly back home with me for a visit when I return to Massachusetts in July. It's my birthday/Green River Festival weekend, and we'll see where things go from there. It is bound to be an epic week filled with family, friends, fantastic music, and a glimpse of a life I want us to have together. A life I know we both truly want, and I believe, both deserve.

I decide to leave my job in Portland in mid-June so I have a month to truly spend time here with the Special Friend. My office gives me a vegan ice cream social party, the CEO takes me to the beautiful downtown VQ spot for lunch, I get wonderful cards from my co-workers, and everyone is sad to see me go. It was quite touching.

After I leave my job, the Special Friend and I take advantage of numerous traveling adventures throughout Oregon thanks to his work, and we are able to spend every night in each other's arms. He calls me his puzzle piece because I fit so perfectly inside of his body cuddling up close.

In bed he constantly gushes about the way I touch him, how close I always snuggle up next to him, and how he loves when I look him in the eyes. He calls me his "Velcro monkey" because I never want to let him leave when he needs to go to work or to his kids. He knows we both want this, and for the first time in a long time, he's positive about a relationship too. He says, "I'm not sure how my life would look without you, and I never want to find out." And then, "You are the absolute sweetest. I love how smiley you've been lately. I've never seen you so happy, and it makes my heart melt when I see you like that." I make sure he knows this is mostly because of him.

One summer night we see Fitz and The Tantrums on the waterfront. As we dance our faces off and kiss, the band starts playing "Out of My League," and he later says every time he hears this on the radio, he thinks of me. I will never hear that song, and so many others we've shared a moment over, and not think of him.

We celebrate the Fourth of July on the waterfront, go to Last Thursdays on Alberta, hike Multnomah Falls, dance up a storm at Kells Irish Pub, go to brunch whenever we like, and just get to enjoy one another. My mom comes to visit again before I leave the city, and the three of us take a trip to beautiful Cannon Beach. My mom, Nomads, Sara, the Special Friend, and I have the happiest sun-soaked times at Portland's famous Waterfront Blues Fest. I can enjoy my friends and this city one last time before leaving. My final month here is filled with many of the best times from this whole Portland experience.

The Special Friend and I talk about the practicality of a bi-coastal relationship and agree it won't be easy. Or practical. And while this scenario is thorny, he *is* a flight attendant. When we first became close, he listed me as his "special friend" for flight benefits. This will be a key factor if our coast-to-coast relationship is to endure.

We plan to fly back and forth regularly to see each other, and I plan to take a short sabbatical from finding full-time work to be able to do this traveling, spend quality time with him when he's in Massachusetts, and write. He continually says he'll do everything he can to eventually move to Northampton, and that he wants it more than anything.

Portland has provided me with many ups and downs, adventures, relationships, and experiences, and I could never have imagined a more potentially fulfilling ending. Except it's not the end with the Special Friend and me, and now it's not even the end between Portland and me. This city could never let me have anything easily or smoothly, and with this powerful romance, the future remains a mystery. The city is still playing hardball with me even as I prepare to leave.

On one of our last bright and lazy weekend mornings in Portland while the Special Friend and I are all cozied up and warm in bed, he looks at me and shivers. His eyes tear up and he says he's having "a moment." He sweetly says, "My heart is just so full of love for you."

We passionately kiss, he grabs my breasts hard, I moan in response, and his face tells me how badly he wants me, how much he craves me, how much he loves me. He growls loud, intensely pinning me down and pushing my arms behind my head on the pillow, every part of our bodies touching. We start to make love. He stares me in the eyes, rubs my cheek, and gives me that adorable smile of his I know had been in hiding before he met me. I feel so happy. I tell him softly, "I am so in love with you." He says louder, "I am so in love with *you*!" And in true Portland fashion, in the window above our heads, the sun fades away and it begins to rain.

EPILOGUE

"**Do not be angry with the rain; it simply does not know how to fall upwards.**"
—Vladimir Nabokov

The Green River Festival welcome home is everything I hope it will be, filled with family from all over New England, scores of friends, rocking live music, perfect July weather, and being in love with the Special Friend visiting me back in Western Massachusetts. The two of us dance under the hot summer sunsets to Brandi Carlile and Gogol Bordello, and he gets along with the many people to whom he is introduced. We celebrate my birthday at two of my favorite spots, Sierra Grille and Tunnel Bar, and I show him the magic of Northampton. He insists that this is really living life.

Throughout this next year after "leaving" Portland, I keep my promise and travel across the country and back virtually every other week to be with him. I survive many days and nights in airport terminals, plenty of those in San Francisco. (It's as if that almost-endless trip home from SFO to PDX, beginning with the Westin getting sick, was foreshadowing my future.) My parents drive through more than one snowstorm, dropping me off or picking me up at Bradley International during the brutal 2014 winter. And all across the country, I become a regular at various airport lounges. From Newark Liberty to O'Hare to SeaTac, bartenders get to know me, and they don't sense I have a drinking problem, but rather a traveling one. They're right. Airport bars aren't really designed for repeat customers.

Then there are the strangers I spend my enroute time with every trip. There's the woman in the Arcata/Eureka breakfast bar who claims she slept with more than one member of The Who back in the day, as she downs Bloody Marys at 9 in the morning while reading Pete Townshend's autobiography; and the random mother in the Washington Dulles jet bridge who leaves me to watch her handicapped daughter in a wheelchair when she goes off to use the restroom. And there's Lindsay, my favorite airport bartender and now a close friend from Laurelwood Brewpub in Portland International, as well as the many men who try to flirt their way into whisking me off to foreign islands when they note my hapless luck at catching flights. I traveled 84,000 miles by plane this year without ever earning a single frequent-flyer mile.

All this airport time is stressful as I sacrifice a lot to be with the Special Friend, and I'm having a tough time finding work, an apartment, and settling into any kind of routine back East as I fly thousands of stand-by miles each month. And did I mention that during our weekend visits we take care of his children at his ex's house while she is elsewhere? I introduce them to Bruce Springsteen, Bob Dylan, and Bunk. I encourage them to have dance parties in the living room, play outside, read books aloud, cook dinner with us, and be more self-sufficient now that they're growing older.

I try to think this is all good for our future. If I give the Special Friend enough time to move the home base for his job closer to the East Coast and figure out arrangements for his kids, we just might be able to live together in Massachusetts. He insists this is what we are working for and it will all be worth it. Plus at least for now, I can still regularly see my friends in Portland and not quite have to say goodbye to the city that keeps pulling me back.

He also visits me in Massachusetts when he can. We fill our time with Celtic music sessions at the Northampton Brewery, autumn beer festivals with beautiful New England foliage as the backdrop, shopping sprees at dusty bookstores, and lots of rock-out music nights with my parents at their home. He fits in wonderfully with my family and friends, especially during the holiday season when we celebrate in Boston. He seems so calm and genuinely grateful when we are together, and there are always tears at the airport when we say hello or goodbye. Our physical and emotional affection toward one another is undeniable.

We are in constant communication, and a typical love text from me reads: "Hi baby, I know we will make this work. I love how we are completely ourselves with each other. I love that you make my day everyday. I love sharing my life with you, and I want to always. You've made me forget all the disappointing men I had in the past, and I only think about being with you. You are the only man I ever notice and want to be with. I care so much for you, and I trust you. I love your funny little quirks, and how incredible our chemistry is. I love spending time with you, whatever we do, and I miss you so much when we are apart. I love you so very much. I can't wait to see you soon."

But here's the kicker: Inexplicably and to my utter astonishment, the Special Friend betrays me and our relationship more deeply and harmfully than I ever could have imagined, doing so behind my back with his soon-to-be ex-wife *and* with other dreadful people he's suddenly surrounding himself with, even as I travel back and forth to be with him.

When we're apart, he lies to me about the relationship with his wife, in whose home he often crashes at (and still pays rent for) when he's not flying. I believe he stays there honorably for his children, even though I know *she* is mendacious and manipulative. He promises me time and again that they have very little communication and never watch their kids at the same time because they can't stand each other. They have an arrangement for being there different nights and weekends, and I remember this from earlier in their messy relationship. He swears on our love and says he's staying far away from all her negativity. Plus her new boyfriend is living with her in the house, and disturbingly they just had a baby together. The Special Friend convinces me that he's at their house as little as possible because he is constantly traveling and working hard. Sounds believable because I trust him, but...

The truth starts to vomit forth via Facebook Messenger on my phone. It comes from his wife, of all people, out of the blue one evening when I am with him in Portland having a night to ourselves. We had just returned to the hotel we're staying in, after seeing Of Montreal at the Wonder Ballroom and having a romantic dinner at the superb vegan trattoria, Portobello. What the fuck is going on?

She informs me that the Special Friend has not been honest with me about their actual relationship. They are attending pool parties together, drinking and singing karaoke in sleazy bars at night, camping in the same tent during a long holiday weekend and, most hurtful, he is telling her intimate details of our relationship. He exposes personal specifics regarding our arguments and the carnal insides of our sex life. Letting someone do whatever they want with you in bed never guarantees that they will treat you right outside of it. I'm learning the hard way.

I literally fall to the floor in disbelief in front of him as I receive and absorb all this over Messenger on my phone. He denies everything, and at first I believe him. Why wouldn't I? This soon-to-be ex-wife has caused immense problems in our relationship before. And she is the one who cheated on him not long ago, dismissing their 10-year marriage with multiple kids by telling him she never even loved him.

I ask him, "Should I write back and call her a liar?" He says, "Yes." I do, and she responds with more confidential information she should not know about us. Then other "friends" of his come forward to me as well, through phone calls, and he is cornered by all the lies he can't find excuses for. He is caught, screams hateful twisted nonsense at me, and tells me that it isn't his problem how I get back home, 3,000 miles away. My heart is shattered, I'm crying, and he doesn't own up to any of it, or apologize. I am in shock. Clearly he is too.

What the fuck is happening? Is this a bad dream? Where has his self-destructive behavior come from? How could I have been so duped into thinking he is someone he isn't? Or is this not really him? Did I do something to bring this on? Did my moving back to Massachusetts cause him to become unhinged? Could it be that he is the most fucked-up and weak of all the people I've ever known, not only from Portland but from my whole life?

The night after I receive these distressful messages from the Special Friend's wife, I meet Nomads at Portland International for a drink at

Beaches Bar, overwhelmed with sadness and confusion and about to leave this place, possibly for good. She is as nauseated as I am about the Special Friend. They had become close during the last couple years, and her wise insights always pointed toward him being one of the good ones. She tries to tell me to just let this whole Portland experience finally go.

She wants to convince me it's time to really move on. We both have tears in our eyes, not only from this recent nightmare but because now we don't know when we'll next see each other. I can't even fathom the hours of traveling that await or, much more seriously, what this means for my future in Massachusetts. Much of what I hoped for is now non-existent and feels, darkly, as if it never existed at all.

Ten days after I return home, I am sitting with my dad on my parents' couch, zoning out with CNN in the background. I'm unfocused these days. I have not heard from the Special Friend at all, not even to see if I made it home alright. My dad suggests texting him to ask what the hell happened, because I need closure of some sort, or at least an explanation. I reach out to him and text, "What happened to my Special Friend?" Immediately he responds with a long-winded text ending with, "My life is completely over without you." I don't know what to think, but my dad assures me that his sentiment should be taken seriously.

Throughout my year of globe-trotting I hear from many of the men I had relations with in these chapters, including the Mister, the Manhandling

Dentist, the South Floridian, even the Soulless Fuck's friends. I don't respond to most of them. Happily the Old Friend, whom I've known since I was 6, and I become closer as he, too, moves back to Massachusetts. I am devastated over the Special Friend, and the Old Friend comforts me in ways I never could have anticipated. I am so grateful for his solace. Nomads meets a man, and I end up being Maid of Honor at their June wedding in beautiful Oregon. My parents fly out, and we spend an unforgettable wedding weekend with Nomads' family from Sri Lanka, celebrating love in a place where it can be so elusive.

During the weeks that follow, I learn of other deceitful things the Special Friend has done behind my back, from various people. Two-faced isn't strong enough to describe his actions. Painfully his lies, built on lies, contradict everything I thought was real. But against all instincts, I can't let go of him or what we planned to have together.

He never cheated on me physically, but emotionally it feels worse on many levels. It's hard to understand, but I hear him out again and again, though I question whether I should. All I ever wanted was openness and honesty from him, and he should have learned this by now from what we both have gone through. I keep up hope that he and I really do have something together, and our communication continues.

Texts from him to me 3,000 miles away at this point are filled with: "The first time I saw you when you walked out of your apartment in Northwest Portland I was blown away that I was going to hang out with someone so incredibly gorgeous. You looked absolutely amazing that night. I fell immediately in love with you after we started talking, and I saw how smart and funny you are. Our personalities clicked so fast which never happens for me with people. Then I continued to get to know you and wanted you so incredibly bad because I was always laughing and forgetting the terrible things I've been through when I was with you. You made me feel good about myself. You made me realize that I deserve so much more out of life. You taught me how to truly live and love. I think about how much I hurt you and us and how much I hate myself for doing that. I think about how amazing it would be to come home to you every night and how that life would look and how badly I want that. I think about the hurt you're feeling every day because of the things I did, and how depressed and angry at myself that makes me feel for making you feel that way. And then I think about how incredibly hard I am going to try for the rest of my life to make up for the things I've done."

How do you forgive someone you can't trust? I'm not sure if that's even going to be possible. Bewildering to myself, I just can't let the time and energy I've poured into our friendship, or the love I still have for him, be drained to nothing. There's a lot of bad to be said about what he did to me, but we had such attachment to one another and so many profound times during these last couple years. I want to believe the Special Friend is different, that deep down he is honest and loving and will do me good.

Throughout my time in Portland, I took plenty of risks with people, and I didn't grant many of them second chances because they didn't deserve them. If I were to ever make an exception, isn't this the man I should do it with? I'm at a crossroads, and moving forward I can't totally give up on him, or on Portland for that matter... at least not yet. For better and worse.

ABOUT THE AUTHOR

Photo by Peter Kitchell

Jessica B. Sokol graduated at the top of her class at Lynn University in Boca Raton, Florida. She currently lives in Northampton, Massachusetts. This is her first book.

Cover photograph by Michael Sokol

Made in the USA
Middletown, DE
30 July 2016